CLOSE EVERY SALE
WITHOUT FAIL

Myers Barnes and Shirley Mozingo

A Service of

NAHB

BuilderBooks™
National Association of Home Builders
1201 15th Street, NW
Washington, DC 20005-2800
(800) 223-2665
www.builderbooks.com

Close Every Sale Without Fail
Myers Barnes and Shirley Mozingo

Theresa Minch	Executive Editor
Jessica Poppe	Assistant Editor
Shirley Mozingo	Copyeditor
E Design Communications	Cover Designer

BuilderBooks at the National Association of Home Builders

ERIC JOHNSON	Publisher
THERESA MINCH	Executive Editor
DORIS TENNYSON	Senior Acquisitions Editor
JESSICA POPPE	Assistant Editor
JENNY LAMBERT	Assistant Editor
BRENDA ANDERSON	Director of Fulfillment
GILL WALKER	Marketing Manager
JACQUELINE BARNES	Marketing Manager
GERALD HOWARD	NAHB Executive Vice President and CEO
MARK PURSELL	Executive Vice President Marketing & Sales
GREG FRENCH	Staff Vice President, Publications and Non-dues Revenue

Cover photo courtesy of Style Solutions, Inc., Liz & Steve Hostetler, Joan & Paul Cain, Bryan Coleman, Veronica & Ed Coleman, Joan & James Gilbert.

ISBN 0-86718-554-6

Printed in the United States of America

Cataloging-in-Publication Data available at the Library of Congress

Disclaimer
This publication is designed to provide accurate and authoritative information in regard to the subject matter covered. It is sold with the understanding that the publisher is not engaged in rendering legal, accounting, or other professional service. If legal advice or other expert assistance is required, the services of a competent professional person should be sought.
—From a Declaration of Principles jointly adopted by a Committee of the American Bar Association and a Committee of Publishers and Associations.

For further information, please contact:
BuilderBooks™
National Association of Home Builders
1201 15th Street, NW
Washington, DC 20005-2800
(800) 223-2665
Check us out online at: www.builderbooks.com

4/03 E Design Communications/Circle Graphics/Victor Graphics 2500

About the Authors

Myers Barnes is one of North America's most sought after speakers and management consultants on professional and business development. In addition to this co-authored book with Shirley Mozingo, he is also the best-selling author of *From Good To Great In New Home & Neighborhood Sales* and *Reach The Top In New Home & Neighborhood Sales*. To increase your company's profits, you may contact Myers at: 252-261-7611, e-mail *sellmore@myersbarnes.com*, or visit *www.myersbarnes.com*.

Shirley Mozingo is a freelance writer and editor living in Manteo, N.C. She writes a weekly real estate column for *The Virginian-Pilot* newspaper and is a regular contributor to a variety of other publications. A former UPI correspondent, she has been a journalist for 25 years. She can be reached at 252-473-4849 or *mozingo@pinn.net*.

Acknowledgments

We gratefully acknowledge everyone who has contributed to the production of this book, both directly and indirectly.

Specifically, we thank the salespeople and managers who have allowed us to share their stories, challenges and successes within these pages.

We are grateful to the editors and staff of BuilderBooks for seeing the value in publishing a book about closing the sale and for getting it "on the shelf" so quickly.

On the home front, our heartfelt gratitude and love goes to Lorena, Hunter, Bill, Michelle, Rick, Chris, Todd, Billy, Suzanne, Ryan, Jacob, Tyler and Hannah. They provided the space, time, emotional support and encouragement necessary when the deadline was approaching and our energy was fading.

And finally we thank you, the reader, without whom there would be no inspiration for writing.

This book is dedicated to those of you who are willing to give your best in a profession that has the best to give.

Happy Sales,
Myers Barnes & Shirley Mozingo

Contents

Introduction

Salesman Red Motley is famous for having said, "Nothing happens until a sale takes place."

Think about that. The salesperson sells cars, tractors, radios, televisions, refrigerators, computers, homes, health and leisure products, ambition and fulfillment. By knocking on doors, answering phones, responding to questions and demonstrating products and services, he or she enriches billions of lives every day.

Without salespeople, there would be no American ships at sea, no busy factories and no jobs. Everywhere they go, they leave people better off.

If we were to stop selling, someone would stop buying. If someone stops buying, then someone else stops making. When someone stops making, someone stops earning. And when someone stops earning, they stop buying.

As a salesperson, you are critical to the productivity and success of this country. In addition, nothing happens for your company until you sell a home or homesite in your community. When you do, everyone—from the stockholders, to the president, to the support staff, to your own customers—benefits.

At the same time, you flip on a switch that activates factories across the world, which determine the direction of the economy.

In 1997, an article in *Forbes* magazine included these calculated statistics: The average American salesman keeps 33 men and women at work—33 people producing the product he sells—and is responsible for the livelihood of 130 people.

Every economic indicator makes reference to the level of sales in a particular company or industry. Our stock market and price indices center around the goods and services being sold at a given time, which means that, as a salesperson, you fuel the entire social and economic process.

Besides powering the economy, you make the American dream a reality. You are involved in what I consider to be the single most important profession in our country. You help people make one of the most significant decisions of their lives—specifically, how they will live.

Regardless of whether your community represents a primary residence, a second home, or a retirement home, you assist people in selecting the environment that will influence and shape their own lives and those of their families.

Before you can help them, however, you may need a little assistance yourself in knowing how to be more effective in new home and new community sales. The purpose of this book is to focus on one specific area of the process—that of closing the sale—because, as Red Motley observed, nothing happens until something is sold.

Within these pages, you will find the knowledge you need to close the sale, without fail. But you should find something else—encouragement.

- Encouragement to target specific goals because, in the long run, you will hit only what you aim for.
- Encouragement to conquer the difficulties that will make you strong and skilled.
- Encouragement to surpass the expectations of others.
- Encouragement to persevere, and not quit.
- Encouragement to take prudent risks.
- Encouragement to find joy within; not with things.
- And encouragement to believe in new beginnings.

CHAPTER 1

The Tale of the Sale

It was a crisp, clear day in November when two couples boarded the 45-foot Columbia yacht and sailed out of the harbor in Annapolis, Md. The yacht had been on display during the annual boat show and they were recruited by its owner to sail it back to its home port in Chesapeake, Va.

Although only one was an experienced sailor, they all had nautical knowledge and were comfortable at sea. They spent a day chartering the course, stocking the galley, preparing for the near-freezing temperatures and testing the ship's electronics. Everything was in order and early Monday morning they cast off, watching the harbor slowly fade into the background behind them.

A few hours into the trip, however, an unexpected storm arose. They had to drop the sails and switch to the ship's engine so they could motor slowly through the churning waters. They had the option of sailing into safe harbors and waiting until the storm passed, but chose to stay on course and make their deadline.

Just before they reached the Intracoastal Waterway in Virginia, the GPS system failed. It was early morning and a thick fog engulfed them. They followed the channel, navigating by a compass, until suddenly the boat lunged slightly and stopped.

Unable to see the channel markers, they had run aground. The boat's keel was firmly embedded in the sand. But that wasn't the worst of it. Because they were still either in the channel or near it, other ships—much larger ones—would be coming through behind them. And the travelers knew that, in the dense fog, their lights would be barely visible.

The four took turns keeping watch. Twice, ships passed close enough to almost touch, but they miraculously avoided colliding with the yacht.

As the sun rose and the fog lifted, high tide returned and they were able to nudge the boat free. They finally sailed into port—safe, tired, thankful, and ready to go again.

My co-author, Shirley Mozingo, was one of those on the yacht. The story is a good metaphor for the new home sales profession.

As a real estate salesperson, you have the power to pilot your career to any destination you choose. Along the way, you'll run aground, encounter unexpected storms, be knocked off course, and probably lose direction.

Although you'll be tempted to seek safe ports, you won't stay there because that leads to complacency and sameness. If this were your goal in life, you wouldn't have chosen sales as a profession.

For you it isn't enough just to be captain of your ship, every ship has a good captain in calm waters. You want the excitement, passion, and rewards that come from meeting challenges and riding the crest. You don't want to travel in a fog, drifting through life in what Theodore Roosevelt called the gray twilight.

> "Far better it is to dare mighty things, to win glorious triumphs, even though checkered by failure, than to take rank with those poor spirits who neither enjoy much nor suffer much, because they live in the gray twilight that knows not victory nor defeat."

As a real estate salesperson, you have the power to pilot your career to any destination you choose.

You could, of course, always remain in the safety of the harbor—never testing the waters, pursuing a dream, venturing into the unknown. But then you would miss the chance to expand your horizons and challenge your soul.

Clearly, there is a risk involved when pursuing goals just as there were risks when the Columbia yacht sailed out of Annapolis. But as President Kennedy commented when asked about the unknown risks of the space program, "We do these things not because they are easy, but because they are hard."

You have chosen new home sales as your career, not because it's easy, but because it dares you to reach the stars and then rewards you for doing so. Although it comes with its share of risks, it also has abundant opportunities waiting to be seized.

In Shakespeare's play Julius Caesar, Brutus says, "There is a tide in the affairs of men which, when taken at the flood, leads on to fortune; omitted, all the voyage of their life is bound in shallows and in miseries."

When the boat and its occupants floated off the shoal, they took advantage of the tide to be lifted out of the shallows. There are tides that ebb and flow through your life daily. How alert are you to grabbing the high ones?

Have You Hugged Your Builder Today?

The beauty of treading into the waters of new home sales is that you aren't sailing (and selling) alone. You have a partner—someone who has offered you a rare joint-venture opportunity.

What's a joint venture? In most cases, a joint venture is a relationship between two people that involves a pooling of resources. In its most common form, it normally is between a person with a lot of money and another person with an idea, drive, and talent.

As a new home salesperson, your builder/developer has presented you with a joint-venture proposition. Basically, he or she has said, "I've got a tremendous opportunity for you with an unlimited income potential. As a matter of fact, the income potential is so incredible that you have the chance to earn an amount that 90 percent of the American population can only dream about achieving.

"I've bought a good piece of land and am about to invest millions of dollars in infrastructure and development costs. Beyond that, I'm going to build hundreds of thousands, if not millions of dollars, in model homes and speculative properties. Of course, I'll further invest in decorating and merchandizing the homes and provide you with a sales office. The office will be fully equipped and I'll pick up all your expenses: utilities, rent, stationary, phones, collateral material, computers, etc. Finally, I'm going to generate your prospects and customers at my expense by creating a website, media ads, billboards, and signs that will help boost your income.

"That's what I'll contribute as part of this joint venture. If you enter this relationship as a salesperson, here's what I expect from you. Show up at work on time, in a respectable car and wearing professional attire. And actively and enthusiastically participate in our sales meetings and company-sponsored training/educational sessions. If you'll do that, I'll put up all the money, take all the risk, and you can earn the income level of the affluent and upper echelon."

What an opportunity! And yet how many salespeople view it that way, much less take the time to thank the builder or developer who offers it to them?

If you haven't thanked your business partner recently, you should. Because he or she has presented you with a fantastic opportunity to choose your lifestyle and chart your future.

Joint-Venture has a Certain "Ring" to It

Many of the world's most successful people got their start in business leveraging off of someone else. They took advantage of another person's capital, expertise, time or assets to get a solid foundation for their own businesses.

Alexander Bell, inventor and founder of Bell Telephone Company, was one of them.

Called Aleck by his family and friends, he was a gifted pianist who learned early how to discriminate pitch. When he was a teenager, he noticed that a chord struck on one piano would echo on another piano in another room. These chords, he realized, could be transmitted through the air and vibrate at the other end in the same pitch.

After Bell married in 1871, he found he needed money to fund research on his new experiment. He had little money himself and his invention sounded so impossible that nobody was willing to back it.

He decided to approach his father-in-law, a successful businessman named Gardiner Greene Hubbard. Bell knew that he would have a tough time selling him on the "impossible" idea of making a voice travel over a wire.

One day, he went to Hubbard's home and sat down in front of the piano. He played some songs before asking Hubbard, "Do you know that I can make this piano sing?"

Skeptical, Hubbard asked him to demonstrate. Bell depressed the pedal, sang *do*, and the piano wires vibrated back. As he explained to Hubbard how he had done it, he described his invention and the principle of voice transmission. As a result, Hubbard backed the project and Alexander Graham Bell introduced the telephone to the world at the Centennial Exhibition in Philadelphia in 1876.

As Bell discovered, selling a good idea takes preplanning and creativity.

Change Your Approach. Don't Abandon Your Vision

New home sales is a profession with an endless series of pitfalls. As a salesperson, you ride an emotional roller coaster that winds between success and failure, taking you to the heights of satisfaction and to the depths of rejection.

I am often asked, "How do you stop experiencing the rejection and frustration of selling?" My straightforward answer is that you don't. They go with the territory.

There's no sidestepping it; the sales profession is filled with challenges. However, it's also full of unimaginable and unlimited opportunities that carry with them the possibility to earn what most of the world considers a dream or fantasy income.

It isn't unrealistic for new home salespeople to expect to earn annual incomes of six and seven figures, and to join the five percent of Americans who are self-made millionaires.

As Bill, a long-time friend, pointed out, professional selling is one of six careers available in this country where you can actually achieve your dreams of earning immeasurable incomes. It also has advantages over the other five professions Bill cited—professional athlete, business owner, physician and attorney, president or CEO of a company, and entertainer.

> *As a salesperson, you ride an emotional roller coaster that winds between success and failure, taking you to the heights of satisfaction and to the depths of rejection.*

Professional athlete. At my height, weight and age, the probability of excelling as an athlete is slim. However, in sales, unlike in sports, genetics, physical attributes, and age do not limit our achievements. In fact, sales is the most non-discriminating profession available.

Entrepreneurs. To operate a business, you need money, good cash flow, and effective management. As management guru Peter Drucker related, "You are only in business as long as your can afford your mistakes." Aside from clothes and cars, salespeople have very limited capital expenditures compared to business owners.

Physicians and attorneys. Many physicians and lawyers go through years of education and hard work to accumulate their fortunes. Physicians today have the additional burden of spending thousands of dollars a year for malpractice insurance to protect their assets. In my case, as well as Bill's, we lacked the educational requirements to become lawyers and doctors. However, as a salesman Bill has consistently earned a six-figure income for years and secured his financial independence.

President/CEO of a major corporation or a Fortune 500 company. Many wealthy people have led large organizations to prominence and were richly rewarded with huge compensation plans and stock options. But now the rules of businesses have changed. Company loyalty is nearly non-existent. Retirement plans can dissolve in a heartbeat. And job security has become buried in an avalanche of overseas competition, company downsizing, and inflated earnings. However, a career in sales promises lifetime security because you are your own boss.

Celebrated entertainer. With reality television shows like American Idol and Star Search, a few everyday people can become famous actors, musicians, or singers. However, it takes marketable talent, perseverance, luck, and knowing the right people who can give you a break. In sales, there is a little song-and-dance that's required to close the sale on a new home, but basically you are alone in the spotlight. You determine the quality of your performance, the rewards you receive, the people you please and the price you're willing to pay.

Just as the other professions aren't suited for everybody, neither is sales. It isn't an easy way to earn a living. And that's good. Because if it were easy, everyone would do it.

When the going does get rough, that's the time to change your approach, not your vision. Make adjustments in the way you're selling but keep your focus on the overall goal of new home sales; and that is *to find out what your customers want and to help them get it.*

No-Frill Closing Skills

So, if sales is a roller coaster of challenges, how do you stay more motivated than frustrated?

You've been to seminars, listened to audiotapes, read the warm-and-fuzzy books, but then real-world challenges broadside you and your motivation evaporates. What happens?

Often, external motivation is a temporary fix and once the cheerleading ends, so does your wherewithal. Internal motivation, on the other hand, is a result of an enhanced feeling of competency—of having confidence in your skills and being best in what you do.

To achieve financial success in sales, you must close the sale. Like any other skill, closing can be learned, mastered and internalized. As you apply the techniques in this book, your competency, confidence and commissions will increase. But not overnight.

You will experience *kaizen*, a word in the Japanese language meaning gradual, constant improvement. It is practiced so faithfully by the Japanese that they have a saying, "If a man has not been seen for three days, his friends should take a good look at him and see what changes have befallen him."

Don't get discouraged if everything doesn't change as quickly as you think it should. Keep applying the principles you learn in this book and watch for *kaizen*.

> *To achieve financial success in sales, you must close the sale.*

Whether you're a seasoned professional or just starting a career in sales, understand this: There is no such thing as a natural-born salesperson. When you took your first breath, the doctor did not slap your backside and proclaim, "Look at this! We have a little salesperson!"

Nor did the doctor make predictions to the parents of the Olympic athletes or accomplished musicians. They achieved greatness by mastering their skills through practice, repetition and application—just as you will.

Let's Begin at the Beginning

Exactly what is closing? According to Webster's dictionary, *closure* is to bring finality . . . finish . . . completion.

As it applies to new home sales, *closing* is the natural ending to a great presentation.

To illustrate, suppose you were attending a music concert. The stage is perfect. The performance is outstanding. As the program concludes, what is the natural ending to the concert? Applause, of course.

Steps of the Sales Process

Closing, prospecting, qualification, presentation, overcoming objections, and following through.

As applause is the natural ending to the musical presentation, so is closing the natural ending to your sales presentation. It is equivalent to finally sailing the yacht into port, docking, and disembarking.

Closing is one of six steps in the sales process. The other five are prospecting, qualification, presentation, overcoming objections, and following through.

The process begins when you find a qualified prospect—someone who has the ability, authority, interest, desire, and need to purchase a new home or homesite—and you deliver your presentation. Your prospect will probably voice some objections and raise some questions during the presentation. You patiently and professionally answer each one before moving to the final step: closing the sale.

You may close on your first try or you may have to return a number of times to ask the prospect to buy. Regardless of when it happens, closing is always the natural ending to the sales process. Without closure, you aren't selling. You're just a guide giving people a tour of new homes.

CHAPTER 2

You Must be Sold Before You Can Sell

Why do people buy? When I ask this to individuals and audiences, I usually get these logical answers:

It was the right price. If a customer really desires the product or service, cost is not a factor. They may think they are shopping price, but they are actually buying based upon their *perception* of value. They will choose to own what they think is the best value, which may not be the lowest-priced home. When buying a new home, clients will not make this significant, lifetime decision based solely on the "right price."

It's what I need. People seldom buy only what they need. In most cases, desire drives the customer to spend beyond his basic needs to purchase what he wants. Our needs are basic and few. Our wants are unlimited and unquenchable. New home buyers, in particular, can easily be upsold. That's where they find a house they can afford to buy, but fall in love with one that's several thousand dollars more. As a salesperson, you must be knowledgeable enough about your new homes and neighborhoods to offer them alternatives that are in their best interests and within their financial boundaries.

It's what I can afford. In this country, many of us tend to spend more than we earn, often to the point of living above our means. With numerous credit cards crammed into our wallets, "what can we afford" translates into "how high is our credit limit."

These Are All Good Reasons to Buy—Or Are They?

Although most shoppers think their purchases are based upon logic—good prices, terms, affordability and quality—the truth is that buying

> *Buying decisions are flushed through emotional channels before ever reaching layers of logic.*

decisions are flushed through emotional channels before ever reaching layers of logic.

Usually high-ticket purchases—such as real estate, furniture, cars, or computer systems—are first made emotionally and then logically. When we see something we want and become emotionally involved before rationalizing our decision to purchase we say something like, "It was the right price" (or) "It was what I needed (or) "It was such a deal I couldn't pass it by."

The purchase is emotional because we're buying intangibles. We think we're buying the product or service, but in reality we're buying the benefit.

For example, *you* sell encyclopedias. *They* buy knowledge. *You* sell insurance. *They* buy peace of mind. *You* sell clothes. *They* buy image. *You* sell computers. *They* buy convenience. *You* sell a heat pump. *They* buy a way to keep warm and cool. *You* sell new homes or homesites. *They* buy pride of ownership and the feeling of satisfaction that your community's lifestyle promises.

Understanding what the customer is buying can mean the difference between success and failure.

Several years ago, Tonka Toys™ introduced a new toy called GoBots®. Since Tonka was already in the market of making trucks, they created a toy vehicle that could be manipulated into a robot. It was an overnight success.

Usually the first new toy of its kind on the market dominates.

> *Understanding what the customer is buying can mean the difference between success and failure.*

However, the following year Hasbro™ introduced a similar toy that drop-kicked GoBots into the stockroom. The reason it was so successful was because the people at Hasbro took time to watch the kids play with GoBots. They learned that the kids didn't necessarily care if the toy started out as a vehicle and ended up as a robot. They just liked the process of changing it.

Hasbro introduced their line of Transformers® and focused the advertising on the process, not the product, because that's what the kids were buying.

In selling new homes and communities, you must tap into the emotional benefit that the home buyer is seeking. The house isn't just bricks and mortar. For that home buyer, it may represent the joy of achievement, the comfort of belonging, the thrill of independence, a pleasurable get-away, childhood memories, or a satisfying investment.

However, before you can sell *them* on the benefits of new homeownership, *you* must be sold.

The Power of Enthusiasm

Around 1930, author and public speaker Dale Carnegie conducted his first class at the 125th Street YMCA in New York City. Attending were fewer than 10 men. One of them, a salesman, had just purchased a country house. He told the class it had been built the autumn before and had neither grass nor landscaping.

Because he had always lived in the city, the man said he wanted a bluegrass lawn. So, during the winter, he burned hickory wood in his fireplace and scattered the ashes across his yard.

"You know," he told the class, "I thought you had to sow seed to get bluegrass. But you don't. All you have to do is to throw hickory-wood ashes on the ground in the autumn and bluegrass will come up in the spring."

Astonished, Carnegie told the man, "If this is true, you have discovered what scientists have been working for in vain for centuries. You have discovered how to take dead matter and make it produce living matter. It just can't be done.

"Maybe bluegrass seed blew in on your land without your knowing anything about it. Or there may have been bluegrass growing there already. But one thing is sure: bluegrass won't grow from hickory-wood ashes alone," Carnegie explained.

The salesman, however, wasn't deterred. In fact, he became more excited, leaped to his feet and exclaimed, "I know what I'm talking about, Mr. Carnegie! After all, I did it!"

Carnegie recalled that the man went on and on, "speaking with enthusiasm, animation and spirit." When he finished, Carnegie asked the class, "How many believe this man can do what he says he can do?"

To his amazement, every man in the room raised his hand. When Carnegie asked them why they believed him, all of them replied, "Because he seems so positive. He is so enthusiastic about himself."

> *If enthusiasm can cause a group of intelligent business people to ignore the basic laws of science, imagine what it can do if someone is actually making sense.*

As Carnegie later pointed out, if enthusiasm can cause a group of intelligent business people to ignore the basic laws of science, imagine what it can do if someone is actually making sense.

What is Enthusiasm?

Well, it isn't a grip-and-grin handshake, hyperactive talking, or leaping around the room. It isn't something you can fake because it comes from within.

As Carnegie explained it, "The way to acquire enthusiasm is to believe in what you are doing, and in yourself, and to want to get something definite accomplished. Enthusiasm will follow as night follows the day."

If you have enthusiasm about your new homes and community, your career, and your company, it will be infectious. Your excitement will ignite the emotions of your prospects and kindle in them a desire to own.

Look at the last four letters of enthusiasm: *IASM* means *I Am Sold Myself.* Unless you become excited about the homes and are sold yourself, nothing will happen. Your prospects will not become emotionally involved until you deliver your presentation with a white-hot excitement that spurs their interest. You must go beyond simply knowing your community/builder/model homes to truly believing in the worthwhile benefits and solutions they offer the buyer.

> *You must be sold yourself before you can sell others.*

Put simply, to show genuine enthusiasm, you must believe in what you sell; believe your prospect will profit by it; and believe in the firm you represent. You must be sold yourself before you can sell others.

Henry Ford attributed his success to enthusiasm. He believed that enthusiasm is the most valuable quality a human being can possess. His famous motto, displayed over his fireplace:

"You can do anything if you have enthusiasm. Enthusiasm is the yeast that makes your hope rise to the stars. Enthusiasm is the sparkle in your eye, it is the swing in your gait, the grip of your hand, the irresistible surge of your will and your energy to execute your ideas. Enthusiasts are fighters. They have fortitude. They have staying qualities. Enthusiasm is at the bottom of all progress! With it there is accomplishment. Without it there are only alibis."

Following a seminar I conducted, an attendee told me she lacked enthusiasm. There were credibility issues surrounding the products and the company she worked for and, to complicate matters, she was disenchanted with the quality of service her company offered.

My advice to her is the same I give to you: If you do not believe in your company, community, and homes—if you wouldn't buy a home yourself or recommend one to your best friend—then you are involved with the wrong neighborhood and builder. If this is the case, have the courage to make a change. Otherwise, you will never develop the enthusiasm needed to succeed and sell your customers. Just as you can transfer positive emotions to your prospects, you can also transfer negative ones.

Picture this. You are holding a plastic eight-ounce cup filled with water. Your prospect walks up with an empty eight-ounce cup. How much water can you transfer from your cup to his? Eight ounces, of course.

Now, imagine that your cup contains only four ounces of water. How much water can you pour into your prospect's cup now?

This is how enthusiasm works. If a sale is a transfer of enthusiasm, you can only pour as much enthusiasm into your prospects as you have in yourself.

> *If a sale is a transfer of enthusiasm, you can only pour as much enthusiasm into your prospects as you have in yourself.*

Great Expectations

Along with enthusiasm, another key quality all top-closing professionals possess is an expectation that a prospect will say Yes if asked often and at the right times.

During a corporate training session for a real estate division of a Fortune 500 company, a top producer for the organization asked, "Myers, does this mean you believe we can actually will a customer into ownership?"

"No," I answered. "But suppose you were in your car driving to your model home. For 30 minutes prior to arrival, you verbally repeated affirmations such as, 'I'm happy to serve by selling. There are many prospects who excitedly await information about my new homes and community.' And all the while, you visualize successfully closing the sale."

"Now, envision another scenario. This time you're driving to your model and you say out loud, "Today will not go well. There probably won't be any prospects who come in and, if they do, all they'll want is to pick up brochures and be on their way.""

Directing the question to the group, I asked which of the two work-day rehearsals would create the mindset for selling a new home.

In unison, the group agreed that thinking positively would because it increases the probability of a sale by affecting the attitude of the sales-person who, in turn, influences the emotions of the buyers.

Henry Ford said, "If you think you can, or think you can't, you are right." Your attitude will create the situation you imagine. You are what you do—not what you say you'll do—and you become what you think.

> *You are what you do—not what you say you'll do—and you become what you think.*

Driving to the model home with the expectancy of a positive outcome does not guarantee a sale; however, it certainly increases the probability of making one.

Often, when I'm conferring with sales-people prior to their appointments, I'll ask them this question to determine their pre-call strategy: "What is it your prospects would like to own," (or) "What do you plan on helping them acquire?"

Usually, I'll receive a reply such as, "Well, I don't think they are ready to own yet. I don't expect them to make a decision today. I'm just giving information at this time."

Do you understand what occurs with this type of mindset? The sales-person's expectation mentally predisposes him to the outcome he expects, which is for the sale not to occur.

I often ask those who attend my seminars, "If everything were perfect and you were shopping for a new home, how many of you would walk into a model home on your first visit and buy it?"

Most of them say they would not do that. So my response is, "If you can't buy it on your first visit, you can't expect to sell it to others on their first visit. And *that* should be your goal."

There are a percentage of home buyers who will buy a home on their first visit. But, because we don't think they will, we ignore the signs, delay the closing techniques, and move on to the next client.

What does it take to conclude a new home sale on the first visit? It takes a shift in your mindset. You don't prejudge those who are dressed poorly. Don't discount those who appear disinterested. Don't reject those driving old cars.

You must believe that there are those who will buy a new home on their first visit and the only way you'll know who they are is to believe that all clients will buy *today*.

When Does a Sale Occur?

It occurs in *your* mind before your *first* sales call. Sell yourself on your new homes and then you're ready to sell others with such enthusiasm that you're convinced they're going to buy.

Every time you meet a prospect, a sale will be made. Either you will sell the prospect on the benefits of homeownership or the prospect will sell you on why he can't buy.

Suffering a Confidence Crisis?

As I said, selling isn't easy. Sometimes our emotional batteries get a little low and we need a boost. Here are ten simple ways to jump-start your self-confidence:

1. Set a realistic goal and reach it.
2. Take a reasonable risk occasionally.
3. List 10 of your strengths.
4. Think positive thoughts about yourself.
5. Avoid replaying mental tapes of your failures.
6. Spend time with people who support you.
7. Meditate daily on small successes.
8. Stay in shape physically by practicing good nutrition, exercising regularly, and getting restful sleep.
9. Schedule a "Dread Day" once a month. On this day, do everything you've been putting off because it's unpleasant. At the end of the day, celebrate accomplishing those things that you've been avoiding.
10. Complete the sentence, "I like myself because . . ."

CHAPTER 3

Acknowledging Fear— Accomplishing Feats

In 1999, on the barrier island of Hatteras, NC, an event took place that many thought was next to impossible. The tallest brick lighthouse in the United States was moved nearly one-quarter mile from its original perch 160 feet from the Atlantic Ocean.

The 208-foot, 2,800-ton Cape Hatteras Lighthouse had stood in that location since 1870, when it was built as a navigational aid for ships voyaging through the treacherous Graveyard of the Atlantic.

Storm-driven waves had eroded the foundation of the sentinel and experts predicted that eventually it would topple into the sea.

A committee formed in 1987 to evaluate and develop options for preserving the Cape Hatteras Light. After many hotly contested debates, the final recommendation was to relocate the lighthouse 2,900 feet to a new resting-place. Nearly 10 years of planning and two years of site preparation were needed to prepare for the move, which was covered in depth by national television.

When the time came, it took 23 days and around $12 million to relocate the lighthouse westward from the ocean's shoreline to a place less susceptible to erosion.

During the sales process, the fear of failure is the biggest obstacle to closing. It affects the salesperson, who fears rejection, and the potential home buyer, who may experience the tensions and negative emotions of buyer's remorse in advance.

If the prospect is not 100 percent certain that she is making the right choice, she becomes a victim of doubt and fear. To avoid closing and to

Fear can erode our confidence just as water erodes our coastlines.

pacify her fear of making a mistake, the prospect makes predictable statements such as, "I'm just looking," (or) "I need to think it over," (or) "I need to discuss this with my banker, accountant, attorney, or family before making a final decision." Although these are the words she speaks, the unspoken message is that she is fearful of making a wrong decision and is feeling buyer's remorse in advance.

As if the buyer's fear isn't enough to stall the sale, there is also the salesperson's fear of rejection. More than anything else, it is this fear of rejection—of asking for a definite decision and risking a negative answer—that keeps most salespeople from achieving their professional goals. And it is this same fear that you must overcome if you are going to experience greatness in sales. As Eleanor Roosevelt observed, "You gain strength, courage and confidence by every experience in which you stop to look fear in the face."

> *"You gain strength, courage and confidence by every experience in which you stop to look fear in the face."*

Why is it that we fear rejection and hearing the word No? Psychologists explain that this fear is rooted in our childhoods. As babies, we entered the world equipped with a repertoire of sensory and perceptual skills but without fears or preconceived notions. We gradually develop knowledge of fear as it is taught to us by our protective or overly critical parents.

You've probably heard the phrase *terrible twos*. In an effort to put a positive spin on this exploratory phase of life, educators today have tagged it the *terrible twos*. Regardless, it is during this stage of a normal childhood that we learned to walk. We were enormously curious, had no fear of anything and wanted to explore and touch everything. Had we not been stopped by a watchful parent, we could have easily been injured or even killed.

Saying the word No repeatedly is how parents train their children to avoid things that have the potential to cause pain. As children approach their third birthday, they will have heard the word No hundreds of times. In fact, research reveals that, by the time the average person reaches adulthood, he or she will have experienced the word No somewhere between 116,000 and 148,000 times. Is it any wonder that, in sales, we want to avoid hearing it?

Does This Sound Familiar?

A person walks into a new community or sales center looking for a home. The salesperson approaches and says, "May I help you?"

The person replies, "No thanks, I'm just looking," (or) "No thanks. I just wanted to see what you have," (or) "Not now. I'm just looking around. If I have any questions, I'll find you."

When the prospect walks in on a mission to buy a new home and the salesperson asks if he can help, the prospect's knee-jerk reaction is going to be, "No. I'm just looking." That's his way of protecting himself and maintaining control.

Salespeople would benefit by understanding that the No they hear from prospects is nothing more than a response mechanism. It's certainly nothing personal.

If you're an average salesperson, you will have as many as four out of five potential home buyers say No the first time you ask. This means that if your closing ratio is 10 percent, you will meet and greet 100 walk-in prospects and, out of them, only ten will become homeowners and 90 will reject your offer to buy. When the economy is down and competition is keen, these percentages increase even more.

So, accept it. As a salesperson, you will hear No many more times than you will hear Yes from your prospects. The Superachiever expects it, prepares for it, and is able to continue forward by enthusiastically responding to objections, building confidence, and implementing well-rehearsed closing techniques.

Remember, if you ask and don't make the sale you're still better off than the salesperson who won't even ask. You may not have a closing, but at least you have closure.

If you ask and don't make the sale you're still better off than the salesperson who won't even ask.

Facing Your Fears

I live on the Outer Banks of North Carolina, not far from a celebrated sand dune called Jockey's Ridge. Located in Jockey's Ridge State Park, the ridge forms the tallest isolated hill of sand on the East Coast.

Thousands of vacationers from all over the world have taken their shoes off and climbed the 90-plus feet to its summit. Some of them strap on wings and go hang-gliding down the side. Others arrive each year and hike to the top to catch the ever-flowing breezes in their kites.

It's such a popular spot that, once a year, there's a kite festival where odd-shaped, lighted, colorful kites blanket the sky. It's soul soothing just to watch.

I mention this to illustrate a point. The kites that vacationers fly off Jockey's Ridge rise *against* and not *with* the wind. In life, as in kite flying, a certain amount of opposition is beneficial. Face it head on and it can help you climb to greater heights in your career.

Here are six strategies to apply when you face the fear of failure head on.

1. **Expect rejection.** This doesn't mean you should have a negative attitude when approaching a prospect. And it doesn't contradict the need for confident expectations. It's just accepting the reality that most sales calls will end with the prospect's refusal or semi-refusal.

What Is a Semi-refusal?

When you are offered objections such as, "I need to think about it," (or) "I'll get back to you later," (or) "I need to discuss this with someone else," and so on.

On the average, more than 80 percent of all sales take place after the salesperson makes five to seven closing attempts. In other words, you must ask prospects to buy your homes a minimum of five to seven times before they decide to sign on the bottom line. What's surprising, however, is that 50 percent of all sales' calls end without the salesperson attempting to close even once.

Furthermore, you may expect many of your prospects to visit multiple communities. Even if they love your homes and lifestyle, they will usually perform "due diligence" by shopping the competition before making their final selections.

If you anticipate the possibility of a refusal, then you can formulate your closing strategies and follow-up campaign.

2. **Don't take rejection personally.** After you understand the prospect's fear of failure, you'll realize that the No that's directed *at you* isn't a rejec-

tion *of you*. It's simply an automatic response initiated by the prospect. Therefore, accept it as a learning experience—an opportunity to fine-tune weak areas in your closing and a chance to practice the true art of salesmanship. Rejection may be a reminder that you need to change direction.

Keep in mind that your prospects' No might be an objection to the home's price, the delivery schedule, contract terms, the neighborhood, the builder or nothing in particular. Unless you have seriously offended them in some way, the prospects are not saying No to you. So don't internalize it. As the expression goes, "It's not all about you."

3. Script, memorize, and rehearse the closing techniques. You build confidence in closing the sale when you know you can respond to any objections your prospects present. The only way to do this is to anticipate their responses and have a closing technique that is scripted, memorized, and adapted to the individual situation. Then their objections won't sabotage your efforts to sell and leave you feeling rejected.

The average salesperson closes poorly because he does not take the time to memorize closing scripts. And he lacks the fortitude and skill to ask for the sale seven times without giving up.

You are familiar with the phrase *art and science*. Closing is a very specific art and science. You cannot practice the art without first mastering the science. Memorization of the technique is the science. After you memorize and internalize the scripts, you practice the art.

Consider a professional actress, for instance. On screen her performance appears effortless. But what is unseen is the scripting and practice that occurs prior to the performance. First, she must practice the science of performance, which is memorizing her script word for word. Then she can apply the art of performance and go on stage.

You do the same, except your stage is the model home or sales center. And your audience is every potential home buyer who walks through the door. To properly perform your role as a professional salesperson, you must be prepared to deliver the information, answer their questions, and guide them to that point of decision.

4. Confront your fears. Ralph Waldo Emerson said, "Do what you fear most and the death of fear is certain." *Confront* your fears. *Control* your fears. But do not take *counsel* with them. They should not dictate your life.

For many, asking for the order once—much less five to seven times—is intimidating. But when you face the obstacles and the fear both flee and you develop faith in your abilities and confidence in your salesmanship.

Expect to feel uncomfortable as you develop your new skills. You're leaving one comfort zone and entering another that's unfamiliar to you, so it's natural to feel uneasy. Through experience you will gain strength, courage and confidence. Then, before you know it, fear will fade like a summer tan.

5. Consider the cost. Why did you choose sales as a profession? Probably because you like the opportunity to have an unlimited paycheck, to be able to be your own boss, to work a schedule that adjusts to your routine and to compete on an even playing field where effort is generously rewarded. If this is the lifestyle you want, then you can't afford to give in to your fear of rejection. If you become timid about asking your prospects for a decision to purchase, then ask yourself, "Am I willing to sacrifice my dream for this fear?"

6. Perceive rejection as success. When facing your prospects, the first commandment is: *Don't let them scare you!* Remember that they are potential buyers. However, they frequently are *indecisive* potential buyers so you are going to receive a certain number of No responses. Expect it. And think of each one as bringing you closer to a Yes.

Dump the Drag

I fly all over the country. Every time I do, one truth is evident. The plane I am on cannot take off if the drag—the air that resists the motion of the plane—exceeds the lift.

To get your sales presentation off the ground, you must help the prospect overcome the drag (the fear of making a wrong decision) while increasing the lift (the excitement of buying a new home).

When your prospects first enter your model home, they are *tabula rasa*, a blank slate. They have not formed opinions about your new homes and community. As you communicate your presentation to them, you will paint a picture upon that blank slate. Use negative words and the picture will be tainted and distorted. Use positive words and your prospects will carry a favorable image of the homes and community.

The words you choose can stir their fears or pacify them. They can motivate a couple to buy their first home from you or drive them out the door and into the model home of a competitor. To paraphrase a song, "They're only words and words are all you have to take their fears away."

Often, indecision and procrastination on the part of the prospect will follow your closing. If you notice this happening, then perhaps the words you have chosen, the information you have shared or the manner in which you've delivered it have not eliminated all of their fears. In this case, you need to work with them to identify what is hindering them from making a decision to buy.

Get a feel for how your closing technique appears to prospects by practicing your presentation *alone* in front of mirror. Observe your facial expressions and what your body language is saying. Experiment with voice modulation, softening it when you are making an important point and pausing to get the listener's attention. Check out your appearance and the statement your clothes, shoes, and hairstyle make about you.

To know the best way to present your new homes and community when talking to potential buyers, refer to the chart below. Listed on the left are negative words that breed fear and skepticism. Replace them by substituting the words on the right, which evoke confidence. (See pages 26 and 27.)

Commit the above power words to your vocabulary and use them as a natural way to present your offer and close the sale. To see what a difference the choice of words can make, review these two approaches to the same closing scenario:

Scene One. The average salesperson asks for the order. "Mr. and Mrs. Walker, this is a great deal and it's our cheapest unit and all that's left. It costs one hundred twenty-four thousand. The down payment is twenty-five grand and the monthly payment is eight hundred five bucks. All you need to do is to sign the contracts to buy it. Well, what do you think?"

Scene Two. The Superachiever asks for the same order in a non-threatening, professional manner. "Mr. and Mrs. Walker, this home is our best value and your final remaining opportunity. The total investment is only one hundred twenty-four thousand with the initial investment being twenty-five thousand, and the monthly investment only eight hundred and five dollars. Mr. and Mrs. Walker, you are making a smart choice for your family, as well as a wise investment. All that's necessary to begin the process is for you to authorize the agreement."

The first scenario creates visions of the salesperson-without-a-clue. It's obvious that he lacks confidence in his homes or is simply lazy in his

Don't Say	Instead Say
Agent. Agent is threatening and provokes a negative thought.	**Representative or Consultant.** To consult is to offer helpful advice and render service.
Buy. To buy is to give up security, which is their money.	**Own, acquire, be involved.** People love to own. They don't like to buy.
Cheaper, cheapest. Diminishes value.	**Best value, less expensive, more affordable.** Reflects smart value consciousness.
Commission. They do not like to pay your commission as part of the purchase price.	**Fee for service.** Your service always outweighs the fee.
Contracts. Sounds stiff, formal, difficult and requires the service of an attorney before signing.	**Paperwork, agreement.** Connotation of mutual understanding.
Complex. The very connotation sounds confusing.	**Amenities or facilities.** "Mrs. Smith, let me show you the exciting lifestyle our recreational facilities and neighborhood amenities offer your family."
Condos, units. Only an amateur would say unit. Represents cold, unemotional structures that are connected with apartments.	**Home, residence or villa.** Pride of ownership.
Cost or price. It always costs too much and the price is too high.	**Total value.** Equates with a fair return on the investment.
Deal. "Make a deal" (or) "Get a deal," sounds shifty. May be too good to be true.	**Value or opportunity.** An investment that leads to a favorable end.
Decision. Final	**Choice.** Optional
Down payment. A request for security (money). Indicates future payments.	**Initial investment.** The beginning of a positive result.
House. Cold and unemotional. A lifeless building.	**Home.** Memories, holidays, warmth, a haven.
Left. Suggests "hard to move" homes or homesites.	**Available or remaining opportunities.** Suggests a planned release, saving the best for last.
Lot. Suggests a tiny parcel or small plot.	**Homesite.** Where they will make the most significant emotional investment of their lives.

Don't Say	Instead Say
Monthly dues, maintenance fees. Has the same impact as paying taxes.	**Monthly maintenance investment or contribution.** Investment toward the integrity of their homes and communities.
Monthly payment. People fear incurring more debt and already have enough payments.	**Monthly investment.** Money toward value and profit.
Pitch. Carnival con man, carpetbagger.	**Presentation.** Introduce an opportunity.
Problem. Everyone has enough problems. Don't complicate the sale.	**Challenge or opportunity.** We rise to the call of a challenge.
Punch list, pre-settlement inspection. Invites them to literally pick the home apart.	**New home orientation.** A time to deliver their warranties and demonstrate how it all works and how they will live, prior to their moving in.
Restrictive covenants. Confining and conveying limited use.	**Protective covenants.** Preserving their investment.
Sell or sold. People do not want to be sold to and do not want you selling to them.	**Help them to own or acquire, Get them involved.** "Mr. Smith, once involved as an owner, you will enjoy the benefits."
Sign. Never sign anything until checking with the attorney.	**Approve, authorize, endorse.** "Mr. Smith, could you authorize the agreement or approve the order, please?"
Spec. The most negative industry jargon. The word "speculative" translates into "built for profit" and opens the door for negotiation.	**Nearly completed or completed home, ground-floor opportunity.** "Mr. Smith, our builder's showcase homes are representations that allow you to experience the quality of construction or give you the opportunity to acquire a completed home right now."
Standard. Nothing special, available to everyone. Implies commonness, blandness, the everyday.	**Included features.** Positions the ordinary to the extraordinary.
Ups, be-backs, tire-kickers. These words are industry slang adopted from the automobile showroom. Let your customer hear, "Sam you're up," (or) "Jenny, your 'be-backs' are here," and you will send them running out the door.	**Customer, guest.** Our business is the customer—to whom we owe our success.

approach. The second scenario reflects a confident salesperson who will probably convert the prospect into a happy homeowner.

Shining a Light on Negatives

When you're being compared to a competitor, enlighten the prospect. The overall rule, of course, is to never knock the competition. Every negative statement you make about your competitor's homes just makes you look bad and reflects poorly on the new home/neighborhood industry.

However, when you are being compared to your competitor, you can use the opportunity to point out that, while they may have deals, you offer value and opportunities. You could say something such as, "In fact, Sam Smith is a good agent and his prices are cheap, but allow me to share with you the lifestyle our community will offer your family and the quality and designs of our new homes."

This is an opportunity for you to develop a unique selling position, which will distinguish your new homes from your competitor's and keep your presentation fresh and original. Tell your prospects what distinct advantages you offer over your competition. Explain why they should choose your community over another and how they benefit by having you as their salesperson.

In trying to lure prospects from the competition, don't promise something you can't deliver and don't be so accommodating that you give away the farm.

Your skill as a salesperson can add to the perceived value of your homes and is a way to differentiate yourself from the crowd of competitors.

A few words of caution here: In trying to lure prospects from the competition, don't promise something you can't deliver and don't be so accommodating that you give away the farm. Remember, you might as well fall flat on your face as to bend over too far backward.

Listen Closely

One skill you can practice that will put you head-and-shoulders above most of your competitors is to listen. What is a good listener? It's someone who looks you in the eye when you're talking and questions you to clarify that what is being heard is what you're really saying.

It's someone who shows concern, is poised, relaxed, emotionally balanced and, during the conversation, reacts with nods, smiles, and appropriate facial expressions.

A good listener pays close attention to what is being said, doesn't interrupt and allows you to fully express yourself on a topic before moving on to another one. And a good listener remembers and uses your name.

Being a good listener can help you overcome a bad case of cold feet when it's time to close the sale. As you listen to your prospects and concentrate on responding to *their* needs, you'll forget about your own. When you look them in the eye, you'll face your fears at the same time.

CHAPTER 4

Selling Is Serving

One of the rules of life is that with every privilege comes a responsibility. The same principle applies in sales. You should consider it a privilege to be with prospective new home buyers. They could be anywhere, but they are choosing to spend time with you. In turn, you have a responsibility to provide them with the information they need to make knowledgeable decisions about buying new homes or homesites.

Therefore, before you attempt to close, you must earn the right to close. There are two essential conditions that must exist prior to asking for the order. Any attempt tó conclude the sales process without meeting these conditions may not only result in a lost sale, but could also be misconstrued as high-pressure selling tactics.

1. The Customer Must Want or Need Your Product or Service

Your responsibility in professional selling is to provide solutions to meet the customer's requirements. If a need for your neighborhood or housing designs does not genuinely exist, or if it is clear to you that what you have to offer will not satisfy the prospects' problems and is not in their best interest, then move on to other prospects.

Before asking for the order, you must have kindled in them a strong desire to buy. Awakening the buying desire—bringing clarity and understanding about the benefits of your community, its locations, and amenities—is the function of the presentation. To prematurely close before arousing sufficient buying desire or before your prospects gain complete understanding of the benefits of owning in your community, will destroy your chance for the sale.

2. The Customer Must Be Able to Afford Your Homes

Your customer should not only have sufficient funds to buy, but also be able to own without being financially strapped. If individuals are sold homes that create a financial burden, they won't enjoy living there and will feel trapped. The pain of making unaffordable mortgage payments will overshadow the pleasure of home ownership.

Whenever my wife and I enjoy dinner out, she invariably seeks the waiter's recommendation. It's not that she lacks confidence in her ability to select a meal; only that she seeks reassurance and knows that he has more knowledge in this area.

In most cases, your customer will seek your recommendation prior to making a home-buying decision. Like my wife, it isn't that the buyer lacks self-confidence, only that he or she seeks reassurance and your knowledgeable input.

You have the opportunity to become an educator when your prospect asks, "What do you recommend?" And you respond, "Based upon your pre-qualification letter from the bank, this particular model would be the best one for you."

If you help your customers by broadening their understanding and knowledge of your homes and community, they will conclude that you're valuable to them because you know what you're talking about and they can trust your judgement.

Sink or Sell

You have the power to turn closing the sale into an exciting and positive event. You can make this happen during your presentation by avoiding these six common selling errors.

1. **Failure to ask for the order.** It's hard to believe, but the main reason people do not buy is that they are not asked to own. Up to 50 percent of all sales calls end without salespeople attempting to close *even once.*

If they do try to close once and hear a No, they drop it, concluding, "I've asked. They've answered. Time to move on."

Researchers have learned that the average sale does not occur until the prospect is asked to own a minimum of five to seven times. Statistics tell another story. In my estimation, even seven attempts is conservative. I would expect you to ask more times, using multiple closing techniques.

The Five-to-Seven Rule

The five-to-seven rule is true in advertising as well. That's the average amount of times a person must see a commercial or an ad before she makes a decision on buying the product. It seems to take the brain that many repetitions before the message hits home.

Only a small percentage of salespeople possess the technical ability and confidence level to ask for the order multiple times. The average, not-so-successful salesperson waits until the end of the presentation then nervously shifts back and forth, timidly asking for the order by saying, "Is this what you had in mind?" or the classic, "Well, what do you think?"

When you ask them what they think about your presentation instead of calling them to action, you're giving them the impression that you are unsure of yourself and your new home community. As a result, their natural response will be, "Well, I think I want to think about it."

You must be eager, prepared, and confident to close. And the more ways you know how to ask, the more likely you are to ask, and the more likely you are to close and earn that commission.

2. **Prejudging the prospect.** Carry this statement throughout your selling career: "Prejudging is not pre-qualifying." Most salespeople try to determine the customer's ability and willingness to own by prejudging. Prejudging usually occurs during the initial moments of the meeting when the salesperson makes a judgement call concerning the prospect's ability to buy based upon his or her appearance, car, mannerisms, or occupation.

Appearances Can Be Deceiving

One day, during a sales meeting, Steve, a top producer, exemplified how salespeople prejudge prospects. His father, a successful surgeon, never reveals his profession when shopping for high-ticket merchandise such as luxury automobiles and real estate investments. He also intentionally dresses down and drives his older car to appear less than qualified. Usually, Steve's father has been able to shop unattended and inconspicuously. Salespeople see him and decide he isn't worth the effort. If he drove his Jaguar and dressed in a three-piece Armani suit, salespeople would have been all over him.

A friend's son, who is a young looking 35 and a $125-an-hour CPA, always dresses casually when visiting potential investment communities for himself and his clients. He says the majority of salespeople look at him and think he can't afford to purchase, so they ignore him. There are two exceptions, however. The salespeople who do approach him are the novice, who is hungry for sales, and the seasoned professional, who knows better than to prejudge and disqualify him.

It is natural that our first impressions are our lasting impressions, but you must resist the tendency to surface-judge people. Ability and willingness to own are not determined by outward appearances.

It should be noted here, however, that human nature being what it is, the prospect is probably giving you the once-over and making a judgement call of his own. So, it is important that you reflect a professional image of yourself and the new homes, company and community you represent.

Another mistake salespeople make during the presentation is deciding that the prospect is contentious because she asks too many questions or he has too many objections. When this happens, the salesperson loses heart and enthusiasm plummets.

Remember that a sale is a transfer of emotion. The moment you decide the prospect will not own is when your energy and enthusiasm dissipate, and you begin delivering a poor presentation.

You'll learn more about the difference between prejudging and prequalifying in another chapter, but for now, focus on not allowing negative impressions to derail your presentation.

3. Talking too much. Most salespeople know *how* to stop talking. They just don't know *when*. They ramble on and on, spewing out information like an open fire hydrant relieving itself of water.

> *Most salespeople know how to stop talking. They just don't know when.*

Mediocre sales organizations focus their training on product knowledge instead of sales methods. As a result, the salesperson's presentation centers on knowledge of the new home community and a lot of memorized facts. Since they know so much, it's natural to tell everyone. After all, this may be the only opportunity the salesperson has to sell this prospect. The problem is that, with information overload, the prospect isn't dazzled but dazed by it all.

Telling is not selling. God gave you two ears and one mouth so you should listen twice as much as you talk. Superior salespeople question skillfully and listen attentively to the prospect's needs. They are patient and show a genuine interest in what the person is saying. Then they ask their way into a sale; they don't talk their way into it. Their words inspire rather than *tire* the buyer.

Telling potential buyers about your new home community is essential to making the sale. But timing is crucial. The information must be spoon-fed to them so they can gradually digest it without choking.

4. Talking past the close. The most valuable instruction my father gave was, "Son, when they are ready to buy, they are ready to buy. So, stop talking and grab your contract."

When you ask a closing question and your prospect confirms he is ready to own, the conversation stops, your presentation ceases and you start preparing the paperwork.

As an example, you might ask, "Current production schedule guarantees delivery by the end of the month. Is that satisfactory?" Your prospect answers, "Yes, it is." At that moment, he has made the decision to own. End your presentation and move swiftly to prepare the contractual agreements.

5. Arguing with the prospect or customer. As the expression goes, "A man convinced against his will, is of the same opinion still."

When a prospect challenges or objects to your claims and you defend your homes, you are in essence telling him that he is wrong. And people dislike thinking they are wrong, even if they are. As humorist Will Rogers pointed out, "Most people would learn from their mistakes if they weren't so busy denying that they made them."

You are in business to win the customer, not a battle. So be agreeable. When customers have objections, respond to them in a positive non-threatening way. Don't be confrontational, antagonistic or walk around with a chip on your shoulder. Avoid giving others the impression that you know it all.

When you're engaged in conversation with your prospects, listen intently and keep an open mind. You just never know when a worthwhile thought might drop into it.

> *"Most people would learn from their mistakes if they weren't so busy denying that they made them."*
>
> —**Will Rogers, humorist**

6. Knocking the competition. Avoid making reference to your competition. If, however, something is said about the competition—negative or positive—simply reply with, "It's a fine company and they seem to do a good job."

If the prospect asks why he should purchase from you instead of the competition, respond with this two-part question: (a) "Why do you feel you should do business with that company?" and (b) "What would cause you *not* to do business with that company?"

Allow time after each question for the prospect to answer. Listen carefully to learn why he would or would not do business with your competitor. This provides you with elements upon which to build your presentation and anticipate objections.

Value-Added Selling

Perhaps you've heard the story of Harry, the owner of a small general-appliance store in Phoenix, Az. Harry was continually dealing with customers who were comparing prices between his store and a nearby discount appliance dealer. He didn't want to knock his competitor, but he was tired of losing sales and customers.

Each time a young couple entered his store with pen and paper in hand, Harry was certain they would ask him detailed questions about prices, features, and model numbers. Then they would head off to his competitor to compare prices.

He would spend an hour selling the customer on the virtues of the appliance only to have them respond, when he asked for the order, "Well, we want to think about it and look around some more."

Harry finally decided to face the competition problem and figure out a solution. This is what he did.

When customers said they wanted to compare prices and shop at some other stores, Harry would nod, smile, move in close and say, "I understand that you are looking for the best deal you can find. I appreciate that because I do the same thing myself. And I know you'll probably head down to Discount Dan's to compare prices. I know I would. But after you've done that, I want you to think of one thing. When you buy from Discount Dan's you get an appliance. A good one. I know, because he sells the same appliances we do."

"But when you buy the same appliance here, you get one thing you can't get at Dan's. You get me. I come with the deal. I stand behind what I sell and I want you to be happy with what you buy. That means I do everything I can to be sure you never regret doing business with me. That's a guarantee."

Harry was practicing value-added selling—giving something extra for the same price. You can do the same. Don't knock the competition. Just offer your customers something your competitors can't—YOU!

How To Know When To Close

Donna, a new home salesperson, approached me one day after a sales meeting and said, "I'm just not sure of the exact moment, the appropriate time, to close. I've scripted and memorized my closing techniques and I understand them. I'm just not sure of the proper moment when I should bridge to the close."

I asked, "Donna what is your favorite part of the sales process; prospecting, qualifying, presenting, overcoming objections, or closing?"

"Oh, Myers, I absolutely love delivering my presentation. I'm so excited about the company and I love showing the property and homes," she said.

"Like you, Donna, most salespeople prefer the presentation portion of the process. It is, in essence, a time for you to socialize. But what you are asking is 'when do I stop socializing and get down to business?'"

"What you are doing is giving the entire presentation and waiting for what you think is the one moment that is most appropriate to close. Donna, the close usually occurs at the end of the presentation, but it has been building all along throughout the presentation.

"It is the process of gaining commitment. You see, there are commitments and minor closes that must occur during the selling process before the prospect makes the major commitment to own.

"For example, you must first gain commitment to agree to an initial appointment, which includes a specific time, location, and date. Donna, as insignificant as this seems, if you cannot gain the commitment and close on something as minor as the appointment, what makes you think you can close something as major as the sale?

"Suppose after obtaining the appointment you assess the needs of the prospect. Now it requires a follow-up call and the need to prepare a proposal. You still have not concluded a sales transaction, so the sale you make is the follow-up appointment. This in itself requires closing skills."

I further explained to Donna, "You are constantly closing and gaining commitments. Commitment and minor-point closings that occur during the sales process could be as simple as determining a need and ensuring your product will satisfy a need. Selling, whether by one-call closing or through multiple-call contacts, is

After or during the presentation the prospect usually has 100 percent of the information available and is more emotionally closer to making a decision than at any other time.

occurring during the entire presentation. *The presentation is actually the process of gaining commitments and closings."*

The most appropriate times to close are during a presentation and at the end of it. You don't put off asking for the order later in the day or week. After or during the presentation the prospect usually has 100 percent of the information available and is more emotionally closer to making a decision than at any other time.

Don't Wait for Warm Fuzzies

I'm not clairvoyant and do not feel that other sales associates are either. Therefore, when salespeople tell me that they have developed a sixth sense regarding closing, I become doubtful about that person's sales ability.

I have never felt my way into closing a sale and don't recommend that you wait until it feels right before you close the sale. Feelings—even the warm, fuzzy ones—aren't dependable.

You can, however, look for certain signs that will indicate the time is right to close the sale. Listen attentively and carefully observe your prospects. They will tell you verbally and physically when they are ready to make the decision to own. If you're especially observant, you can almost see them waving the green flag signaling you to go ahead and ask for their order.

Inquiring Minds Want to Know

Usually, prospects will want to nail down answers to some questions before making a final decision to buy.

They may ask for your recommendation. When the customer asks your opinion, he is only looking for calm reassurance from you and a recommendation. "Mr. Smith, based on all the information you have provided, I would suggest your needs would best be met by the XYZ model. We could begin construction within 30 days and have your brand new home delivered to you in 120 days. That would meet your needs perfectly, wouldn't it?"

The most visible verbal clue when the sale involves a couple is when a husband and wife look at one another and ask, "Honey, what do you think?" When this happens, assume the sale is complete, congratulate them on making a decision to own and move into the *Handshake Close*, which will be explained later. Don't wait for the partner to say, "Let's think about it."

They may question you about the home's features and options. The prospect will say, "We are really interested and would like to own, but we want a home on this particular homesite."

Tell them you'll check availability. Then say, "Mr. and Mrs. Prospect, I'm not sure that choice homesite is available for immediate release. Would you like me to check?"

If one of them says yes, to "call or check," then find out if it is available and, if so, say, "Good news, Mr. and Mrs. Prospect. There is just one available and I've placed it on hold for you while we process the paperwork."

At this point, one partner may ask, "If I buy, would you include a certain option at no additional cost?"

You respond, "Mr. and Mrs. Prospect, I'm not sure if that's possible. However, why don't we put in writing what you would like and if it's accepted, then it's just additional value. Let's prepare the paperwork based upon your request, shall we?"

They will ask about delivery. "How soon can I move in?" is a frequent buying question. Use it to ask a closing question. The answers you get from the prospect serve two purposes. First, they confirm the prospect is serious. Second, they cause the person to tell you he's making the decision to own.

So, you reply, "Mr. Prospect, if we proceed forward today, we may be able to deliver it within 90 days. Is that satisfactory?" Or you can ask, "How soon do you need it?" When the prospect suggests the time frame, cease your presentation and attempt to conclude the sale.

They want you to repeat details. "What about your warranty, or tell me again what features are included with this home?" Whenever the prospect asks you to explain something a second time, he is indicating that he is approaching the decision to own. Initiate a *Summary Close* and repeat all the features and benefits followed by an invitation to own.

They question price or terms. "What about financing?" she asks.

You reply with something like, "Have you prearranged financing or would you like me to handle the details?"

If she says, "The price is higher than I expected," you say, "Mrs. Prospect, suppose I could offer you terms that would fit within your budget."

Questions concerning price and terms offer the perfect opportunity to close. Be sure to answer all buying questions with a response that either confirms ownership or leads the prospect into ownership.

They ask about value. The prospect may say, "How do I know this is the best price or do you negotiate price?"

When asked this question, it is pretty clear he has reached the buying decision and decided to own. So, it's time to offer assurances, move to the *Paint A Fantasy Picture Close* and wrap up the details.

"Mr. Prospect, you have received the absolute best value. Your family will enjoy neighborhood amenities for years to come. By the way, will you be taking title in both your names?"

Silent Speech

You're familiar with the expression, "What you do speaks louder than what you say." It's imperative that you carefully observe your client's body language and actions throughout the presentation to get an accurate read on what she or he is silently saying. Here are some non-verbal clues to spot:

The customer calculates the numbers or reviews the contracts. He is beyond thinking about it and is financially justifying the decision. Whenever he reaches for his calculator or asks you to determine the monthly investment and how much the new home is going to cost, it's time to close. Also, when the prospect reviews the contract, it's time to close. Say, for example, "Mr. Prospect, do you have any questions before we begin the paperwork?" The prospect answers No and you proceed with the paperwork. If he answers Yes, simply encourage him to verbalize his final questions or objections.

The couples' attitude changes. They have fought or acted tense all along, but suddenly they become happy. With a husband and wife as prospects, the non-verbal clue may be that they touch one another or hold hands. When prospects start to feel good about the decision to own, they sometimes begin to relax, smile, laugh or suddenly become friendlier.

The customer asks for a second showing. In real estate, the presentation includes the showing of the property. When the customer asks to go back out for another viewing, this indicates he is ready to proceed forward. In this case there is no proper place to complete the paperwork. Usually, upon a second view, the prospect is emotionally high and contracts can be completed outside the office or sales center. Many contracts have been completed on car hoods, kitchen tables, in restaurants and so on.

The customer's posture changes. The prospect, who has been leaning back, will suddenly sit up straight or lean forward. Whenever someone's physical posture changes, it usually indicates he's made a decision. So, move forward and ask a closing question. "Mr. Prospect, the initial investment is $5,000 and can be secured by cash or check. What would be more convenient for you?"

Many salespeople become so involved in the presentation part of the sales process that, if the prospect decides to buy during the presentation, they literally will not interrupt the presentation to let him. Don't become so enthralled with the sound of your own voice that you miss the buying signals indicating that the customer is ready to own.

> *Don't become so enthralled with the sound of your own voice that you miss the buying signals indicating that the customer is ready to own.*

Do You Have What it Takes?

In the mid-1990s, the Harvard Business School conducted a study to determine the most common characteristics of top salespeople. What they learned underscores the fact that most people can be top sellers if they are willing to study more and to concentrate on improving their performance.

The attributes were:

- **Above-average willpower and determination.** Although they were tempted to quit, they persisted toward their goals.
- **Did not take No personally.** They did not allow a decline to purchase make them feel like a failure. They had enough confidence and self-esteem to allow themselves to be disappointed, but not devastated.
- **Above average ambition and desire to succeed.** This affected their priorities and governed how they spent their time.
- **Ability to approach strangers, even when they felt uncomfortable.**
- **Intensely goal-oriented.** They knew what they wanted and how much progress they were making in achieving it. This straightforward focus prevented them from becoming sidetracked. As the expression goes, "You can judge the size of a person's goals by what he lets distract him."
- **Total acceptance of responsibility for results.** They didn't try to blame their customers, their company, the competition or the country's economy for their shortcomings. When sales dipped, they dug in harder to sell.
- **High levels of empathy.** They had the ability to place themselves in their customer's shoes and to identify with what their needs were.
- **Completely honest with themselves and their customers.** Regardless of the temptation, they told it like it was.

5

Qualify Buyers First

Changing Your Perception About Rejection

Your goal in professional selling is to determine each home buyer's needs and financial ability, to offer solutions, and to conclude the transaction as soon as possible. However, before you are able to lead your prospect through to close, it is essential to qualify all potential owners.

If you are tempted to ignore this critical step, remember that the sale initiates with the buyer who can make the decision. Therefore, it's reasonable to conclude that investing time with qualified buyers produces a higher sales volume.

Research has shown that two-thirds of the presentations given by salespeople today are wasted on individuals who are not qualified to purchase. Considering this, is it surprising that sales can be frustrating?

As logical and sensible as it is to qualify prospects, many salespeople still fail to do so and immediately launch into their presentations, assuming that they know the needs of their customers. The result is that the salesperson becomes discouraged and frustrated because he or she doesn't understand why so few sales are closing.

The fact is you simply cannot conclude a new home sale with an unqualified individual. Before you ever begin the paperwork, you must do your homework. Spend time asking questions, listening to the answers, and determining if your prospects really like the new home/homesite; if they have a desire to own in your community; if the location is convenient; and if they have the money, desire, credit history, and authority to purchase.

Do this first and you'll close more sales and have fewer rejections.

Why Should You Pre-Qualify Prospects?

Pre-qualifying determines wants, needs, and desires. The majority of home buyers today feel most community salespeople are insensitive and uncaring. They mistakenly conclude that their top priority is simply making the sale at whatever the cost. Period. They do not feel we truly care about providing the right homes for their specific needs.

Qualification is a process of discovery that benefits the new home salesperson and the prospect. By asking questions, you discover their true agenda and can focus on reality rather than the prospect's perception of reality. This will simplify and facilitate the home-buying process for both of you.

Pre-qualifying provides you with the prospect's financial status. Once you determine if their needs can be satisfied by your community and the area in which it is located, your next priority is to discover whether the prospect has the financial ability to take advantage of your new homesites and homes. If financial resources are not adequate, then there is no reason to waste their time or yours.

By asking the right questions and not forming hasty conclusions based upon exterior circumstances (such as their appearance, automobile, clothes), you determine where your prospects stand financially and if they can afford what you're selling.

As the authors learned when they wrote *The Millionaire Next Door*, there's a new breed of millionaires today who live well below their means, don't drive flashy cars, and dress conservatively. They choose not to display their social status, which makes it difficult to identify one who's shopping for a new home.

The bottom line is that you can't judge a book by its cover and you can't judge people by their trappings. To find the value of both, you must take time to discover the inside information.

Pre-qualifying provides you with the prospect's financial parameters. You don't want to oversell or undersell the prospect. By pre-qualifying him, you can present and demonstrate the homes and homesites that are within his financial boundaries and property needs.

If you present a $40,000 interior homesite to a $150,000 golf fairway customer, you will frustrate the prospect and probably lose the sale. On the other hand, if you present a new half-million-dollar home to a customer whose financial ability is a quarter of a million dollars, you risk alienating the prospect and losing the sale.

Pre-qualifying determines which parties are involved in the decision to own. There's nothing more frustrating than to knock somebody's socks off with a dynamic presentation; have a transaction mentally and emotionally wrapped up; and then be told that the sale is contingent on someone else such as a partner, a spouse, a parent, child or business partner. If you find that all parties are not available for a presentation, then deliver an overview of your new home community and reschedule the complete presentation for a time that better suits everyone's schedule.

Pre-qualifying determines the time frame. It is essential that you know when the prospect is willing and able to take advantage of your offer. Determine whether she wants to purchase today, next week, a month or a year from now.

Pre-qualifying reveals the competition. When you pre-qualify, you learn about the other neighborhoods and builders who are competing for the same customer. It allows you to structure your presentation with your competitor's product, services, and prices in mind.

Pre-qualifying helps eliminate objections before they arise. If you question skillfully and listen attentively, prospective purchasers will tell you everything you need to know to help them with their home-buying decisions. By asking the right questions, you allow the prospect the opportunity to talk about herself and her concerns. As you listen, you'll not only absorb valuable information but you'll also be able to determine if she is preoccupied, impatient, disinterested or indifferent.

> *Skillful questioning allows you to extinguish areas of concern before they even become objections.*

The more you know, the better you can accurately respond to objections. But even better than that, skillful questioning allows you to extinguish areas of concern *before* they even become objections.

Controlling the Fear of Pre-Qualification

Even though the process of pre-qualifying a prospect is important, most salespeople avoid it. Why?

Beyond fearing the process itself, the average salesperson perceives he or she will be viewed as an intruder probing into the prospect's personal space and soliciting information about their needs, wants, desires, financial resources, and authority to purchase.

However, the reality is that you cannot help potential home buyers with the most significant emotional and financial decisions of their lives until you properly understand their needs and financial status. And the only way to do that is through a question-and-answer conversation.

Pre-qualifying is simply the part of the sales process that is a sharing of knowledge. Basically, you are saying to the prospect, "I know all about the community and these new homes and homesites. You know all about you. When we combine this information, we will have enough knowledge on which to make a solid decision that will be in your best interest. Now, you go first. Then I will be better equipped to match my property to your preferences."

Don't Travel Through Life on a Banana Peel

If you have problems controlling the sales process and influencing your prospect positively, you probably fell like you're sliding through life on a banana peel. Your workday is unbalanced and you just can't seem to find solid footing or get control of the situation.

In nearly every meeting of two or more persons, there is a dominant person who controls the conversation. In sales, the person in control of the circumstances and conversation should be you. And it can be if you remember one thing: Someone in the group will always make a sale. Either you will sell the prospect on your new homes/community or the prospect will sell you on why he can't buy/look/close right now.

The Five Areas of Pre-Qualification

The five basic categories to identify before beginning your sales presentation, demonstrating your new homes/community and concluding the sale are:

1. **Area.** The number-one consideration your prospect will have while shopping for a home in a new neighborhood is the area. Regardless of how dazzling your presentation is and how glorious your community and its homes are, customers will not own in a geographic area that does not fit with their values and emotional agenda.

When selling new homes, you must sell from the *outside in*. The average salesperson sells from the *inside out*. He rushes the home buyer out to see the new homes and homesites first, then talks briefly about the community with no regard to discovering why the prospect wants to be located in the particular geographic range where the neighborhood and homes are located.

Think for a moment. If someone were to ask directions to your home, would you first give them your street address? Probably not. You would begin by telling them the name of your county or city of residence, then tell them which neighborhood you live in, and finally your street address.

Potential home buyers like an overview first. Once they picture the surrounding area, then they are ready for more specific information.

Have you ever had a potential customer view your homes and then say, "I wish this home was in another community" (or) "We love the neighborhood, but we are too far from work, school districts, shopping, facilities, etc."?

Outside-in selling requires that the salesperson recognize that people don't just live in homes. They live in particular areas within the confines of the neighborhoods in which their homes are located. Consider the following:

▍ For year-round communities, the distance to work, schools districts, a church, and synagogue, medical facilities, and shopping areas are the top priorities in the prospect's mind.

▍ In resort/retirement communities, the challenge may magnify. These buyers are searching different states for property. So, you must first determine if your state is right for them and if their preference is for a new home in the mountains, along the coast or inland. If you're selling resort/retirement communities, remember that the hottest prospects are those who have previously visited and/or continuously visit your area because the repeat visitor is already sold on the location.

2. **Time frame.** How urgent is the need? How soon can the appropriate person(s) take advantage of your sales opportunity? The time frame is critical. It determines the sales presentation, urgency, follow-up procedures, and when you are able to close the sale. It also dictates when you will be paid.

You will find time frame and financial resources normally will coincide with one another. For example, if a prospect says he is 90 days, six months or a year into the future, you will find there is a condition—such as selling his home—that prohibits the immediate sale.

3. Financial resources (money). This is a crucial category. Your prospects may want or need what you're offering, but if your neighborhood and homes are not within their financial parameters, they won't qualify for a loan.

It is important during this phase to be able to differentiate between the prospect's wants and needs. I've represented luxury second-homes in oceanfront and golf course communities. Interior homes, without an ocean or a fairway view, sold from $450,000. Oceanfront homes ranged in price from $800,000 to more than a million dollars.

Without fail, everyone who viewed the property would choose to own the oceanfront or fairway properties. Yet, my sales team and I understood that, although everyone wanted the premiere properties, only a select few could afford this luxury. The majority of our sales were interior homes because of their affordability.

Even though most buyers may want oceanfront or fairway property, if they don't have the financial resources to buy it, then their decision to purchase must be based upon what they need, not upon what they want.

Also, a new homesite or home will usually require bank financing so you may need to qualify your prospect in two separate categories.

- **Down payment or initial investment:** To borrow money, you must have money. When financial terms are offered, banks or financial institutions may require the customer to have a position of equity. They want the buyers to be *at risk* with them.
- **Monthly payment or monthly investment:** Your prospect must qualify financially to afford the monthly investment. Reputable banks require a customer to meet specific debt ratios in proportion to income. In other words, banks will only allow a certain amount of debt to be incurred by the customer.

4. Authority. Who will be responsible for the purchase decision? Will you be able to follow up, secure, and deliver your presentation to all persons involved in the decision to purchase?

Don't delude yourself. In the case of a couple buying a home, there are always two people involved in the decision—both husband and wife or two significant others.

Today, many couples shop neighborhoods using the "process of exclusion." One person first visits the community alone to cross it off the list or validate it for the other person. After narrowing down the selection of desirable new home neighborhoods, the other partner will then arrive to look over the ones that have been prescreened and selected. Obviously, attempting to close the sale without both decision-makers present will result in no decision or a delayed decision to own.

Often, with resort real estate, I have been involved with partnerships, joint ventures, and syndicates that purchase investment properties as a group. In most cases, I met first with one individual who assured me he was the decision-maker, representing the interest of the entire group.

In the early days of my career, I was gullible and believed this was true, so I would give presentations and attempt to conclude the transaction with one person verses the entire group. I quickly learned that, when several investors are involved, all partners pertinent to the decision to own must be present. One of the greatest errors a salesperson can make is to believe the prospect when he is told, "I make all the decisions. Just tell me what it is you have to offer."

5. **Wants, needs, and desires.** The key to qualifying a customer is not information dumping; it's information gathering. Therefore, qualifying may have an intimidating, even judgmental tone associated with it. Yet your initial goal should be to question your prospects so you can create your presentation around what is best for them.

Although rapid-fire questioning may be necessary in high-traffic new home communities, in general your questions should be presented in a conversational—not confrontational—manner. Otherwise, you risk giving customers the impression that you are trying to determine if they are worthy of your time.

If, however, you learn that the prospective buyer has no desire for your neighborhood, its location, the homes or he lacks financial resources, then simply cut your presentation short, exit gracefully, and press on to the next opportunity.

Information Gathering

I once shared this technique of gathering information with an outstanding salesperson who sold many high-ticket items. Barbara told me her sales soared after she started asking two simple questions: "How pressing is your need?" and "When do you plan to take advantage of my service?"

If You Don't Ask, They Won't Tell

Why ask questions? Because it's the only way to get the answers you need to better serve your customers.

When you pre-qualify your prospects by asking specific questions, it helps you:

- Understand your prospect better.
- Lock in on the prospect's needs and how they relate to a new home or homesite.
- Know why it's important to meet those needs.
- Establish a warmer relationship with the prospect by practicing the law of reciprocity, which is a mutual exchange of information.
- Create a more professional, caring impression because you're a more informed salesperson.
- Determine the prospect's buying power.
- Recognize who all the decision-makers are.

- Learn about your prospects' passions and motivations in purchasing a new home, including what they expect from the builder and the neighborhood.
- Identify any unreal expectations the prospect may have about the homes, amenities, location, delivery schedule, and price.
- Establish yourself as a consultant and a trusted advisor who has their best interests in mind.
- Place prospects at ease. Remember, they are naturally uncomfortable when they walk into your model home or sales center. This is unfamiliar territory to them and they probably view you as someone who is eager to sell them something at any cost. By engaging them in relaxed conversation, you can ease their anxiety, and allow them the luxury of transitioning into a receptive frame of mind.

Is There Intelligent Life in Your Emotions?

For decades, psychologists have told us that our intellectual intelligence (measured as IQ) is an accurate indicator of how successful we will be. They assumed that people with a high IQ would accomplish more and go further in life.

In the 1990s, however, researchers found that this isn't necessarily true and that a person's *emotional intelligence* might be a better predictor of success.

The term *emotional intelligence* was introduced in 1990 by Dr. John Mayer as a "type of social intelligence that involves the ability to monitor one's own and others' emotions, to discriminate among them and to use the information to guide one's thinking and actions."

Emotional intelligence is about developing a sense of self-awareness, of having empathy for others and of handling relationships in a harmonious way. It's about not jumping to conclusions but getting the whole picture before you react. It is understanding your emotions and those of others and then acting in the most appropriate way based upon that understanding. People with healthy emotional intelligence aren't fearful of making life-altering decisions, setting boundaries, meeting goals and communicating with others.

Researchers believe that people with high emotional intelligence will be increasingly valued and perceived as an asset in the workplace.

As a salesperson pre-qualifying prospects, you activate your emotional intelligence *prior to* tapping into your intellectual intelligence. You spend time learning all you can about the prospect *before* sharing your knowledge of new homes and communities. That way you'll be more empathic about your prospect's needs, eliminate parts of your presentation that aren't applicable and direct your prospects to the new homes or homesites that are best suited for them.

> *Believe in what you do and your belief will make it true.*

By asking questions, you connect with people on an emotional level first and get the whole picture before deciding the best course of action. It's all part of social development and emotional competence, two components necessary in relationship selling.

So, don't be timid or embarrassed when pre-qualifying your prospect. Instead, act bold and self-assured. Believe in what you do and your belief will make it true.

What to Say When You Don't Know What to Say

To guide your prospect through the sales process, you must learn how to control the process (not the prospect) by using scripted dialogues.

Here are some scripts to memorize that will help you learn where your customers are so you can help them get to where they want to be in new home ownership. They cover the five categories of pre-qualification: area, time frame, financial resources, authority, and wants/needs/desires.

PRE-QUALIFYING SCRIPTS

Area

Superachiever: "Bill, Mary let me give you a brief overview of our community. As you see by our map, we are located (geographically). You will notice we are only ____ miles from the school district, a few minutes from the areas best shopping center."

Superachiever: "Oh, by the way, in looking at this aerial photograph, where are you presently living?"

Superachiever: "Why are you considering moving to the area?" and/or "Why are you considering a new home?" Is it the school district? Is it the shopping? Is it convenient to work? Is it to move out of/into the city?"

NOTE: From your area map, you would then progress to your community map to create an immediate sense of urgency.

Superachiever: "Mr. and Mrs. Prospect, before discussing our amenities you will notice on our community map the homesites that are tagged/flagged in red. This indicates the homesites that have already been sold. As you can see, we are quite busy at (community). As a matter of fact, we have ____ homes/homesites that are purchased daily/weekly by families/people just like you."

You may consider pausing for a response or continue with:

Superachiever: "Mr. and Mrs. Prospect, you are going to love (community). As you can see by the number of homes/homesites that have been sold, everyone loves our homes/community. We tell all of our customers that it's not a matter of whether you will fall in love with our community/homes/homesites. It's really a matter of once you do fall in love with our community/homes/homesites, as fast as they are selling, will we have what you are looking for?" (or) "Will we be able to have your new home built as soon as you need it?"

For Buyers of Resort/Retirement Communities

Prospect: "We are just beginning to drive the coast."

Superachiever: "Bill, Mary, let me give you a brief overview of our community. As you notice by our aerial map, we are located in (state). In driving the coast, you will have several states to select from." (a) "Have you narrowed your choice of states?" (b) Have you decided whether you would prefer mountains, inland, or the coast?"

NOTE: Your best prospects are those who have either visited or vacationed in your specific state/county/town. This means the first sale (area) is made. If they are unfamiliar with your area, you must make two sales. First, sell them on your area and then on your community.

From your aerial map showing neighboring states, progress to your town map and point out the medical facilities, shopping, etc. From the town map, go to your community map to create an urgency to buy and to present your amenities.

Time Frame

As mentioned earlier, you must determine if there is a reason your prospects cannot buy a home immediately.

Script One

Superachiever: "Ms. Prospect, how soon have you thought of making a move?" (or) "How soon before you invest in your new home/homesite?" (or) "How soon before you plan on moving into your new home?"
Prospect: "Probably six months."
Superachiever: "Really! What will be different?"
Prospect: "I'll have sold my home."
NOTE: On the surface she seems to be unqualified. Continue to probe.

Superachiever: "I'm curious. Is it that you need to sell your home or you would just feel more comfortable if you sold your home first?"
Prospect: "I would just feel more comfortable."
NOTE: By probing you may have taken what initially seemed an UN-qualified prospect and helped her realize that she may be qualified to purchase now. Keep probing.

Superachiever: "I guess what I'm asking is, if you found the perfect property at the ideal price, would it be necessary to wait until your home sells or would you take advantage of the right opportunity if it came along today?"
Prospect: "If it were the right opportunity, I guess I could move."
NOTE: By probing, you have taken what initially seemed an UN-qualified prospect and proven to yourself and to her that her time frame may not disqualify her from purchasing a new home now.

In the event the prospect says she must sell her home first, proceed with the following script.

Superachiever: "Ms. Prospect, I'm curious. Is it you must sell your home or would it just feel more comfortable if you sold your home first?"
Prospect: "No, I have to sell my home."
NOTE: Probe and further qualify the prospect.

Superachiever: "I understand. Have you listed your home?" (If she has listed her home ask:)
NOTE: If she answers No, she is too far into the future. Focus on a qualified prospect.

Superachiever: "Great, how's the market." (Or, if the prospect is renting) "How soon before your lease expires?"

Script Two

Superachiever: "I'm curious, how long have you been looking at new communities/new homes?"

Prospect: "Just this week." (or) "Six months." (or) "Three years."

Superachiever: (Pause between each question to await the answers) "What communities/homes have you looked at? What did you like best about (community)? What did you like least? What kept you from investing? What are you still looking for?"

Script Three

Superachiever: "Mr. Prospect, there are only two considerations in regards to real estate and your investment time frame. The two considerations are price and availability. First, you can feel certain whatever is available today will probably be gone tomorrow. Secondly, in all probability the values will increase. I'm wondering, have you noticed increasing values and diminishing availability in your shopping process?"

Financial Resources

When qualifying financial resources, home buyers often start with a preconceived notion of how much they would *like* to invest versus how much they *will actually* invest. In other words, *willingness to pay* and *ability to pay* are two separate issues. New home buyers initially shop "logically" but buy "emotionally." They seldom stay within their budgets. Use these scripts to determine the true investment range by employing the two words "up to."

Script One

Superachiever: "Mr. and Mrs. Prospect, what investment range are you considering with your new home/homesite?"

Prospect: "About $180,000."

Superachiever: Respond quickly and curiously with "up to?"

Prospect: "Maybe $200,000 to $250,000."

If your prospects change their investment position, then you have learned the true investment range. If they do not change their investment range, they may respond by saying something like:

Prospect: "There is no 'up to.' We've settled at $180,000 period."

Superachiever: "I understand. At the same time, not wanting to perform a disservice for you, if there were a particular home/homesite that was $5,000 to $10,000 more than your investment range, should I show this home to you or is $180,000 your absolute ceiling?"

Script Two

Superachiever: "Mr. and Mrs. Prospect our homes range from $_____ to $_____ and would require an initial investment of only $_____. Have you set that amount aside?" (or) "Have you made arrangements for the initial investment?"

Script Three

Superachiever: "Congratulations on the sale of your home/home-site. How much did you realize from the sale that you will be rolling over to your new home/homesite?"

Script Four

Superachiever: "Mr. Prospect, have you secured your financial arrangements or would you like me to handle the details for you?"

Script Five

Superachiever: "Mr. Prospect, have you been to your bank yet?"
Prospect: "No."
Superachiever: "Could I make a suggestion? We have wonderful relationships with many outstanding financial institutions. As a matter of fact, let's make an appointment now, regardless if this is the community of your choice. At least this way you'll know exactly where you stand."

NOTE: Securing the appointment has several advantages. (1) It allows you to sell a home on a contingency basis prior to their bank visit. (2) It assures the continuing appointment. (3) It temporarily takes them out of the market by forming a business relationship with you.

Authority

Your goal is to quickly determine who the decision-makers are. This creates a challenge because of nontraditional relationships, so you must delicately discover who will be living in the home.

Superachiever: "Ms. Prospect, how many people will be enjoying your new home?"
Prospect: "Four."
Superachiever: "Outstanding … and that would be?"
Prospect: "My children and significant other."
Superachiever: "How many bedrooms will you require?"
Prospect: "I guess four."

Superachiever: "Your bedroom plus two children equals three bedrooms. I'm curious, how would you use the fourth room, as a home office, den, or guestroom?"
Prospect: "As a home office."
Superachiever: "Ms. Prospect, we have two phenomenal homes/floor plans that include four bedrooms, including one that can be used as an office. Let's go take a look. Oh, by the way, when can we assemble everyone together to see your new home?"

Wants, Needs, and Desires

Your strategy is to help them determine their hot buttons so when you progress to the demonstration/site selection portion of the sales process, you only show properties that satisfy their emotional agendas as well as their financial parameters.

Superachiever: "Mr. and Mrs. Prospect, have you specifically decided on a particular floor plan? What I'm really asking is do you know how many bedrooms and baths you want?

The customers may respond "Yes." If so, ask them to describe their new home. Should the prospects respond by saying "We don't know" (or) "We're just out getting ideas," then ask:

Superachiever: "What type of home do you have now?"

Patiently wait while they describe its features, number of bedrooms, kitchen, baths, dining area, yard, etc. Being creatures of habit, they may want many of the same features in their new home.

Superachiever: "Your home sounds wonderful. May I ask if there is anything about your home that you would change or improve?"
NOTE: This should bring you to their true hot button.

Pre-qualifying Non-Committed Buyers

Frequently, you will have visitors who are "just looking" and curious to see the model homes and how they are decorated. Do not discount this prospect. Countless homes have been purchased by those who were "just looking." Once a spectacular design or amenity-packed community has sparked discontent, a great salesperson can help the *now dissatisfied* homeowner explore the possibilities of new home ownership.

Superachiever: "Mr. and Mrs. Prospect, how long have you lived in your present home?"

Regardless of the answer, follow up by saying, "I'm sure it was a great investment. I'm curious though. Knowing what you know now, is there anything you would change about your home?"

Allow them to elaborate.

> **Superachiever:** "How about your neighborhood? Has it changed and developed the way you originally anticipated?"

If they express discontent when they answer, you are in a position to proceed with your presentation.

> **Superachiever:** "Mr. and Mrs. Prospect, that's why so many people just like you are relocating to (community). Let me give you a quick overview and you will discover for yourself why so many new home buyers want to live here."

Pre-Qualifying First-Time Homebuyers

Frequently, first-time home buyers may have a "phantom buyer" (parent, relative, friend) in the background. The following script works well if the phantom buyer is a Realtor® or another expert who is advising them.

> **Superachiever:** "You are fortunate to have someone so knowledgeable help you with your selection process. Let's set up a convenient time to meet around both of your schedules so (the advisor's name) can experience first hand why you are so excited about the opportunities at (community).
>
> *NOTE: When you secure the appointment, realize the advisor will play a critical role in the final decision. Regardless of how much time you have invested with your prospect, you must start back at the beginning and go through the entire sales process with their advisor.*

Pre-Qualifying Partners in Real Estate

This script is primarily for resort real estate sales. But beware. Normally when a partner, such as a relative or friend, is necessary, it's a sign of a financially unqualified prospect. Your strategy is to determine the qualification of one buyer independent of the other.

> **Superachiever:** "Bill, Mary, I'm curious. If Jan and Mike were unable or not interested in owning this property after you all view it, would you be in a position to proceed forward?"
> **Bill and Mary:** "Yes."
> **Superachiever:** "Jan and Mike, if Bill and Mary were not interested in owning this property, would you proceed forward?"

Jan and Mike: "I'm not sure." (or) "No."

NOTE: You now know if Jan and Mike fall in love with the property and Bill and Mary do not, you do not stand a chance of selling it. Conversely, if Jan and Mike do not like the property, then Bill and Mary are still viable prospects. This being the case, you may consider separating the two couples so the disinterested or unqualified prospects will not negate the interested party's decision to purchase.

Become a Rejection Specialist

Pre-qualifying is a process that will continue through the course of the entire sales process. By asking questions in advance, you can decide if this is a qualified prospect or what he or she needs to become one.

Changing your perception about rejection. In the beginning of this chapter, you learned that experts concur that as many as two-thirds of today's sales presentations are delivered to nonqualified buyers. With this thought in mind, ask yourself these two questions:

▌ Now that you have been made aware of the five categories of pre-qualification, have you been guilty of giving presentations to non-qualified buyers?

▌ Can you have an abundance of appointments from qualified and unqualified prospects and be successful?

If you have been in sales for any period of time you have probably heard that sales is a numbers game. If you put yourself in front of enough people, a certain number will purchase. This is not necessarily true. You can have unlimited traffic and still not be successful, especially if your presentations are given to those who are not qualified to buy.

Often, salespeople experience rejection because they fail to qualify their prospects, not because they fail to demonstrate their new homes and community. This results in anxiety and discouragement, which could be reduced or eliminated by positioning themselves as the one who decides whether or nor to continue with the presentation.

Most salespeople see the customer in the driver's seat with the power to *eject* and move on, *reject* the salesperson or accept the offer. It shouldn't be that way. You, the salesperson, should be the virtual chauffeur, mapping out the territory. and delivering your prospects to their home-buying destination. The reality is that you can be the one in control if you take the time to qualify your prospects before launching into your sales presentation.

A Doctor of Sales

Doctors always diagnose before they prescribe. Prescription before diagnosis would be malpractice.

Presentation before qualification is sell-malpractice.

As a salesperson, you must diagnose (discover the condition of your prospect) before you prescribe (offer a solution). Presentation before qualification is sell-malpractice.

Invest 10 to 30 minutes of your time in prequalifying your customers and stop wasting hours, days and maybe months delivering presentations and attempting to conclude sales with those who cannot—or will not—buy a new home from you.

One Final Thought

There are signposts along the road of life. When one has deceived you, do you lengthen your stride or look for a place to sit down?

Sometimes a prospect will deceive you. If this happens, will you become discouraged with the process and sit at your desk for a few days licking your wounds? Or will you try harder to discover the truth the next time?

There will be prospects who paint a rosy picture, tell you what they think you want to hear or deliberately deceive you. That's just part of doing business. When it happens, remember that you can't control what others tell you, but you can control your reaction to it. Adversity of any kind can break you or cause you to break records.

CHAPTER 6

Take Exception to Objections

You can't be in sales without expecting prospects to voice their opinions and ask questions when buying new homes. When you hear their objections, you shouldn't perceive them as roadblocks obstructing the sale. Instead, think of an objection as a bend in the road. Every bend that you encounter allows you to turn a corner and head off into a new direction.

There are many reasons prospects will interrupt your presentation with an objection. Sometimes, they are beginning to experience a fear of buying or of making a mistake. They may have concerns that you haven't addressed or be seeking validation for their own thoughts. Regardless, each time they present an objection and you respond to it, it allows you to share more information about your new homes and community.

So, objections shouldn't concern you. What should concern you, however, is if you deliver a dazzling presentation and your prospect sits there stone-faced throughout and doesn't offer one objection or question. Often, prospects who do not object—who do not challenge your homes and the claims you make—do not buy.

It's time to take exception to objections. Don't perceive them as negatives. Instead, be thankful for the opportunity to defend your homes and clarify your pricing when the prospect questions them.

Take a lesson from the Internet. The goal of each website is to keep you logged on as long as possible. Because the longer you are on the site, the more likely you are to buy what it's selling. Internet marketers call this "stickiness."

The same principle applies in one-on-one sales. The longer you keep your prospect in conversation, the more likely he is to make a decision to purchase that new home. Each time he expresses an objection or asks a question, it gives you a chance to extend the conversation.

> *The longer you keep your prospect in conversation, the more likely he is to make a decision to purchase that new home.*

Research has shown that even prospects who respond in an abrasive manner may be doing so because they are becoming emotionally involved in the sale. So, don't be discouraged, offensive or upset.

Instead of ignoring or avoiding objections, welcome them for what they are—bends in the road that send the sales presentation in the direction the prospect needs to go in order to make an informed decision about buying.

How Objections Benefit You

Objections often mean your potential buyer needs more information. When she says, "I need to think it over," she is really saying, "I am not yet convinced and need additional information to be certain of the decision."

If she says, "I need to talk this over with my accountant, attorney or a third party," she is saying, "I'm not yet certain; I need approval and assurances."

When she says, "The home is too expensive or I can get one cheaper elsewhere," she wants you to prove that you offer the best value. "I do not like the color," means "What other colors are there or can you get me the color I want?" And, of course, the response "I'm just looking" means she does not yet have enough information to make a buying decision.

In order to address her concerns and guide her to the point where she can make an informed decision, you must listen to the objections but look for the meaning behind them and respond accordingly.

Objections are your signposts. Input from the prospect provides you with critical path markers to follow. Objections represent concerns that must be resolved during your presentation in order to close the sale. Whatever issues the prospect challenges are those that are most important to him and, therefore, should be important to you. Provide him with enough knowledge and he will probably become a new home buyer.

Objections indicate interest. A lack of objections from your prospects can signify a lack of interest. Normally, if they do not have the financial ability to own or have no interest in your homes or community, they will react to your presentation in one of two ways.

▌ They will appear unemotional and slightly bored, without responding to anything you say. They may sit with their arms crossed over
their chests, which is a defensive posture. To evaluate their level of
interest and to break through the "armed" barrier, you can pass
them something they must reach for and hold, such as pictures of
the homes, a fact sheet that illustrates what you're saying, testimonials from other home buyers, builder information, etc.

▌ The second disinterested response you may get is when the
prospect comments, "Yes, it sounds great," throughout the presentation. That's a ho-hum reaction intended to politely show you that
she's listening but not participating in the conversation. You may
want to stop the presentation and solicit some feedback from her.

When is an Objection a Condition?

There is a difference between an *objection* and a *condition*. Before you can
complete your presentation effectively and close the sale, you must
understand which one you are hearing from the prospect.

An *objection* is nothing more than an unanswered question.
Somewhere in your presentation you have either said something or failed
to address an issue that has left a question in the prospect's mind. It rat-
tles around in his subconscious until he decides it's time to toss it back as
an objection. The good thing is it's something concrete you can address
and overcome.

When you hear an objection, you can assume the prospect has one of
the following concerns:

▌ There is something you said that the prospect did not understand.
▌ There is something you said that the prospect does not believe or
questions.
▌ There is something the prospects are trying to hide. They have not
been forthright in giving you all the facts about their qualifications.

To get more in-depth information from the prospect and to help him
identify the real reasons he is objecting, respond by saying one or more of
the following:

▌ "Thank you for bringing that to my attention. Do you have any
other concerns?"
▌ "I can see that this is a serious concern of yours and I'll address it.
Could you tell me if this is the only problem that's keeping you
from making a decision to buy a new home?"

▍ "It's interesting that you feel that way. Do you mind my asking why you question it?"
▍ "Other customers have expressed that opinion. May I tell you what they decided?"
▍ "It's interesting that you say that. Perhaps there's something you haven't told me that would make a difference in your ability to purchase a home."
▍ "Would you mind sharing with me the reasons you feel you cannot buy a new home right now?"

Some of the answers you'll receive from prospects may be *conditions* rather than *objections*. Unlike an objection, a *condition* is an obstacle. It is a barrier or situation that prevents a prospect from buying.

For instance, a prospect says, "I cannot make a decision without my wife/husband." That's a condition you cannot get around. You must deliver your presentation to all decision-makers prior to moving forward with the sale.

Or the prospects may not meet the financial criteria. Perhaps they have the funds available for the initial investment but, because of past credit history, cannot obtain a loan. Maybe they can afford the monthly investment but are cash poor and do not have adequate funds for a down payment.

Conditions usually require some form of action that must be taken by the *prospects* before they can purchase a new home. Even following a brilliant presentation, you won't be able to close the sale because they aren't qualified to buy until they improve or remove this *condition*.

Show Them How They Can Afford the Home

After an intensive workshop I had conducted with about 150 new home salespeople, Alex approached me and said, "I hear what you're saying about the difference between conditions and objections. But I sell a rather pricey community and so prospects frequently tell me that they can't afford to buy a home here. I've already prequalified them. I know they have the budget and the financial resources. So, what can I say when they object on price?"

"Alex," I replied, "what your prospects are really wanting is for you to show them how they can afford the new home. So, you overcome their objection by offering them terms that fit within their budget."

Often, conditions become a Cinderella in the sales presentation. They are unjustifiably neglected and repeatedly pushed aside, as Cinderella was in the fairy tale. Don't make this mistake. If you don't acknowledge the condition and deal with it, you'll end up wasting time and getting frustrated. You won't satisfy the customer. You won't get to close and you won't collect your commission.

Since conditions are "statements of fact" regarding your prospect, it doesn't matter how good you are, how developed your skills or how great your answers, you are not going to circumvent a condition.

What's interesting is that most prospects initially feel their *objections* are conditions. They think that, when they offer the objection, they are presenting you with an obstacle that prohibits them from buying.

When a Prospect Says it Costs Too Much

Author and motivational speaker Zig Ziglar suggests this response when a prospect says it costs too much: "The price is high. I don't think there's any question about the price being high, Mr. Prospect. But when you add the benefits of quality, subtract the disappointments of cheapness, multiply the pleasure of buying something good and divide the cost over a period of time, the arithmetic comes out in your favor. If it costs you a hundred dollars but does you a thousand dollars worth of good, then by any yardstick, you've bought a bargain, haven't you?

I've found this approach is especially applicable in resort real estate sales where there may be seasonal rental income to offset the mortgage, providing another benefit to new home ownership.

The bottom line is that, before you can close the sale, you must identify and/or eliminate objections and conditions. *Objections* usually are a disguise for questions and more information. Answer them to the customer's satisfaction and close the sale.

Conditions will become evident when you pre-qualify your prospect, so don't skip this step and you shouldn't encounter a condition as the reason for not closing the sale.

You Don't Need a Crystal Ball

Since the dawn of the first sales call, salespeople have been hearing, "I need to think it over," (or) "The home is too expensive," (or) "I need to review the matter with my brother's niece, whose son is an accountant."

Objections Are Forever

I can see it now. Back in the dinosaur days, there were cave sellers in three-piece reptile suits scribbling their sales projections on cavern walls. An ad in the Rock Hard Times brings in a couple wanting to buy a new cave in a neighborhood that isn't overrun by the Spinosaurus family of meat-munching lizards.

"Good morning," the cave seller says. "I saw you pull up outside and may I comment on how much I like your new set of wheels."

"Thanks," the cave dwellers reply. "We saw your ad for the new Camarasaurus Cave model and thought we'd stop by and check it out on our way to play Jurassic miniature golf."

The cave seller takes the time to pre-qualify the dwellers and deliver a solid sales presentation. At the conclusion, he tells the dwellers that the cost of the new cave will be ten mammoth skins.

"What!" they exclaim. "Ten? Well, in the next hollow, they're only asking eight mammoth skins and they're throwing in a free Webbfoot Grill so we'll be ready to cook when fire is discovered. We'll have to think this over and get back to you."

These comments are nothing new. And yet it still surprises me how many salespeople are caught off guard when they hear them. Unfortunately, many a salesperson has tossed the prospect a brochure and said, "Call me after you've thought about it if you're interested in buying."

That's a way to run off customers but it's no way to run a business. Here's a better alternative. Since all objections are predictable, you can plan your responses in advance.

Like a Broadway actor, you can memorize your lines (*presentation*) and know the lines (*objections*) of the other performers (*prospects*) before the action even begins.

As I tell people in my seminars, "You know what they are going to say in advance. Since you know this, your strategy must be to plan your responses ahead of time."

You don't need a crystal ball to do this. All you need to do is apply the "Law of Six."

What is the "Law of Six?"

In sales, there is a universal axiom that sales trainer Brian Tracy calls The Law of Six. It states, "Customers really have no more than six objections to own in your neighborhood."

It may seem like you hear countless objections to buying. However, if you categorize them, you will find they normally fall into six basic categories.

In my resort real estate business, for example, the six objections we heard regularly from prospects were:

- Location (area)
- Competition
- Performance (as to claims)
- Finance
- Third-party approval
- Square-foot home pricing

After identifying the objections, we developed ironclad scripted answers to them. After we armed ourselves with airtight answers to these predictable objections, the company set new sales records.

The point is that you cannot wait until you are involved in the presentation and then try to make up an answer. To close more sales, you must take a proactive approach, not a reactive one.

Your job as a professional salesperson is to discover for yourself, or with your sales team, the six common objections you hear consistently. Once you've identified them, write down what your responses should be and memorize them.

> *To close more sales, you must take a proactive approach, not a reactive one.*

Confront Objections

Back in the days of black-and-white television, there was a western adventure show called "Have Gun, Will Travel." It starred a black-hatted, suave character who was an educated soldier of fortune with an eloquent sense of morality who sold his gunslinging services to the highest bidder.

Potential employers were handed his business card. On the top line was printed his name, "Paladin." And just below it was a simple statement of fact: "Have gun, will travel."

Not to suggest that you should wear black and carry a gun, but there's something to be said for singleness of purpose. When it comes to confronting objections, your statement should be: "Have Answers, Will Talk."

Whose Objections Are They Anyway?

The objections you hear from your prospects are the easiest to overcome. Those that you hear in your own mind are more difficult.

All of us have mental tapes we play, rewind, and replay. Sometimes they remind us of mistakes we've made and can't seem to forget. Or they may replay painful conversations or unpleasant experiences.

These imaginary tapes can fast-forward across your mind when you're in the midst of a sales presentation, raising doubts and eroding your confidence. Sometimes these tapes carry unsettled issues pertaining to your new homes/community. Perhaps you're uncomfortable with the prices or terms of the homes or you are uncertain about the credibility of the builder or the amenity package.

Regardless of what it is, if you're not convinced that your new home community is the best value available, you won't be able to convince others. When you are ready to close and there's a final objection about price or terms or credibility, you'll replay your own doubts. Since you can't convincingly overcome an objection you agree with, you'll probably lose the sale.

If this happens, you must invest the time and get enough information to put your doubts to rest or find another community to represent. You have to be 100 percent sold on what you're selling or you'll transfer your doubts to your prospects.

Activate an Attitude Adjustment

Maybe you just need to change your attitude about sales in general. How can you do that? The same way you change anything else in life.

- **Begin by beginning.** Don't wait until everything is "just right" or until you "feel like it." Start now. Identify the area that needs improvement, roll up your sleeves and get going.
- **Keep an open mind.** Try to understand why you're experiencing doubts, why you're having questions and when they began. Keep your antenna up to locate areas of weakness and solutions. Talk to others discreetly. And don't discount their suggestions and ideas.
- **Start simple.** Don't feel pressured. Get an honest feel for what's bothering you. Validate the information and your feelings. Take time to analyze and pinpoint the problem(s). Make certain that your opinions are based upon reality and not on your *perception* of reality.

▌ **Keep improving.** Once you've located the areas that are bothering you and settled on solutions, keep digging. Explore your mind. Are there other areas of discomfort reflected in your sales presentation? What else do you need to "sell yourself on" before you can sell others?

Harboring a Hidden Agenda

Frequently, the sale is stopped by one final objection that is actually comprised of several smaller objections.

Either consciously or subconsciously, your prospect is aware that, if he gives you this hidden objection and you answer it, he will have to move forward in the sales process and seriously consider purchasing the new home.

For whatever reason, he wants to avoid this position so he holds back a final objection, camouflaging it behind a smoke screen of minor ones.

When you sense the prospect is hesitating and hiding behind a smoke-screen objection say, "Mr. Prospect, I sense a bit of hesitancy. Do you mind my asking what it is?"

If you remain silent, the prospect will answer. But, regardless of his response, reply with, "That's a great question, I'm glad you asked. In addition to that, is there anything else that would prohibit your proceeding forward?" Again, the key is to be silent and allow him the opportunity to answer.

If the prospect responds, "No, that's all," then you have arrived at the final objection. If, however, he is still voicing objections, then continue asking, "In addition to that, is there anything else?" Do this until you are confident that all his objections have been aired and answered.

After the final objection, say, "Mr. Prospect, I understand what you've told me and it makes perfect sense. Now, what will it take to satisfy your concerns?"

The Just Suppose Close

The *Just Suppose* method of closing is also referred to as *Handling the Final Objection Close.* You have led the prospect to the point where he obviously wants and needs your home or homesite, but the final objection is causing him to hesitate.

With the *Just Suppose Close,* you remove the final reason for not continuing.

If the prospect says, "I'm just not sure you can deliver my home as quickly as you say," then you reply, "Mr. Prospect, I understand how you feel. *Just suppose* for a moment that I could satisfy all of your concerns in writing. Is there any other reason that would cause you not to buy today?" At this point, he must either say No or reveal the real reason for not proceeding forward.

This is the perfect method for blowing past a smoke-screen objection and uncovering insincere objections. By incorporating *Just Suppose,* the prospect will either agree or lead you to another, and possibly final, objection.

It is imperative that you remain perfectly silent and listen to all his concerns. Afterward, you may consider employing the closing technique of *Subject To* or *Conditional Terms* selling.

Use the *Conditional Terms/Subject To Close* after you have arrived at the final objection and the prospect says, "I need to check with my banker."

You reply, "Mr. Prospect, that makes perfect sense. Prior to speaking with your banker and to facilitate the transaction in a timely fashion, let's prepare the paperwork now and make the sale subject to your banker's final approval. This way we can start the process and if, by chance, your banker does not agree with your decision, then we will simply start over. That makes sense, doesn't it?"

You will never be closer to concluding the sale than at the very moment you arrive at the final objection. Instead of having him come back at another time and of taking a chance on the prospect's fears setting in and his emotions diminishing, ask for the order now.

Stop the Mental Flip-Flop

The *Mental Flip-Flop* is the prospect's psychological justification for purchasing a new home. If the prospect makes the mental switch to that of a customer, then he psychologically enters into the process of justifying all the reasons he will become an owner. If you leave him thinking about the home as a non-owner, the opposite occurs. He does not think of reasons to go ahead with the sale but dwells on his fears and all the reasons he should not own.

Always attempt to conclude the transaction at the moment you answer the final objection and take the prospect out of the market, even if it means making the sale subject to conditional terms. Then, when you two revisit to satisfy the conditions, he is returning as a customer who has bought instead of a prospect who has been thinking about it.

Positively Answer Objections

Discuss and answer all the objections tactfully, delicately and with a positive attitude. As mentioned earlier, an objection is just an unanswered question in a prospect's mind. Treat the question as a request for more information.

When you are offered an objection, remain calm and non-argumentative, welcoming the objection. Remember, it will be impossible to move into the closing sequence until you have answered all questions and concerns. Therefore, you want the prospect to feel free to continue objecting until there are no more concerns.

Say, "Mr. Prospect, I'm glad you brought that up," (or) "Thanks for bringing that up," then answer each objection.

> *An objection is just an unanswered question in a prospect's mind.*

Feel-Felt-Found

Another way of handling an objection is with the *Feel-Felt-Found* method. It's based on creating a strong perception that you are understanding and empathetic. It also employs the closing technique of third-party testimonial endorsements.

For example, the prospect says, "I can get it elsewhere for less," (or) "I'm not in the market."

You respond, "Mr. Prospect, I understand how you feel. Many others just like you felt the same way initially, but once they became an owner, this is what they found. . . ." Then elaborate with a third-party testimonial about someone who was in the same situation or circumstances as they are in, but as a result of going ahead with the decision to purchase, they experienced great success and happiness.

If the objection is price, warranty, service or any other concrete concern, the phrase, "I understand how you feel" sends a strong message to the prospect that you truly care. Follow-up with a third-party endorsement from a happy customer, reinforcing the prospect's decision to proceed forward with the purchase.

When the prospect says it's too expensive, you can respond, "Mr. Prospect, I understand how you feel. I recently had a customer who was in a similar situation and felt the same as you. However, what he found as a result of owning was, although the price seemed initially higher, our service and warranties far outweighed the value our competitor could offer. Tell me, is price your only concern or would reliable service and extended warranties also be important considerations?"

By sincerely being empathic to the prospect's feelings and providing third-party testimonials, you can extinguish most objections.

Take Six Steps Forward

There are six basic steps for handling objections and addressing prospects' questions and concerns. The renowned sales trainer J. Douglas Edwards popularized this system.

Step 1 Really Hear the Objection

Do not interrupt, but listen entirely and attentively to the objection. Give the prospect the opportunity to express his or her emotional concerns without interruption. Although you may have heard the same objection one thousand times before, it is the prospect's first time expressing it to you.

Step 2 Repeat the Objection Back to the Prospect

This is a critical step. It often helps the prospect answer his own objection when he hears it repeated back to him. State the objection out loud in a kind, non-threatening way.

When the prospect says, "It costs too much," repeat it back as a question: "It costs too much?" Parroting, as it's called, has several benefits:

I It puts the ball back in his or her court so you can get more information.
I It makes your prospect feel important and understood.
I It verifies that you heard the objection.

Step 3 Question the Objection

Remember the first objections you hear may be masking a larger one. So, ask for elaboration. "Mr. Prospect, let me clarify my thinking or let me be sure I understand you correctly. If it were not for (objection), then would you proceed forward today? Is that right?" Remain silent and let him answer.

Step 4 Answer the Objection with Your Preplanned Response

Once you're certain that you've ferreted out the whole story behind their final objection, you can cite your memorized response with confidence, clarity, and concern for the well being of the prospects.

Step 5 Confirm that the Objection Does Not Block the Sale

You have answered the objection, but you now must confirm that the objection is no longer a reason for the prospect to avoid becoming a buyer.

"That answers your question then, doesn't it, Mr. Prospect?" (or) "That makes sense to you, doesn't it?"

If the prospect is not satisfied with your answer, now is the time to know. You cannot move forward and close until you are certain the issues are put to rest. If the prospect is satisfied, move to the final step.

Step 6 Close

It is important to understand that handling objections and guiding the prospect to close are occurring simultaneously. As you overcome each objection, you move closer to the close.

> **Superachiever:** "Well, Mr. Prospect, do you have any additional questions before beginning the paperwork?"
> **Prospect:** "No."
> **Superachiever:** "Congratulations! I'm excited for you. By the way, will it be both your name and your wife's name appearing on the agreements?"

It's How You Play the Game

As golf pro Jack Nicklaus says, "It's too late to practice your game when you're on the course."

In sales, the time for *preparation* is before the *presentation*.

Vince Lombardi of the Green Bay Packers was one of the most triumphant coaches in football history. His secret to success? Over-preparation.

Lombardi knew that many professional events are won during the final two minutes of the game. So, he required his players to practice five quarters and not the usual four.

> *"It's too late to practice your game when you're on the course."*
>
> —Jack Nicklaus,
> golf pro

During the final quarter of a game, when the opposing team is wearing down, the Packers still had enough energy to play another quarter. They were mentally and physically conditioned to go the extra mile.

You, too, must be overly prepared. Plan ahead for those objections so they won't wear you out and eliminate you from the playing field.

To become a Superachiever, apply the four "Rs:" Rehearse, review, respond, reward.

Rehearse your scripts out loud. *Review* them in your mind until they are memorized. *Respond* promptly when you hear a prospect object. And enjoy the *reward* of having a satisfied customer and a commission check.

CHAPTER 7

When Is a Prospect Not a Prospect?

A prospect is a prospect until you close the sale. At that point, the prospect becomes a buyer.

Closing the sale is the final step—and the ultimate goal—in the sales process. Without it, you would accumulate a lot of prospects but no paychecks.

Before getting into the specific closing strategies you can implement, here are some closing tips.

Use Your Memory and Memorex

Once again, the professional salesperson is like an actor who must memorize the script before going on stage. In this case, your script consists of (1) the answers to prospects' objections and (2) different types of closing techniques.

The professional salesperson is like an actor who must memorize the script before going on stage.

Why should you memorize this information? Because it makes closing a sale and signing a new home contract go a lot smoother.

On a bigger scale, however, there's another reason. What you remember, what you consider significant, what you value in life, and what you eliminate from your past all combine to define who you are. Although this is your history, it influences your future because it can affect your dreams, confidence, relationships, and goals.

How Should You Memorize Your Sales Script?

The brain works similar to a computer. When it determines that information needs to be saved, it places it in your memory files. Your short-term memory is like your computer's desktop. From here, you can quickly retrieve recent information and access long-term information stored in the gray matter or cerebral cortex of the brain, which is comparable to your computer's hard drive. The key, of course, is to file information in the hard drive that is beneficial and easy to find.

Tips from the Experts

Here are some tips from the experts on enhancing your ability to remember and retrieve information that you've memorized.

- **Don't let your mind be absent when you're memorizing.** There are three stages of learning: registering the thought, filing the thought and, retrieving the thought. If you don't pay attention when you're memorizing something, then the thoughts aren't registering. When you go to retrieve the information, it won't be there. So, pay attention. It affects retention.

- **Eliminate distractions and try memorizing just before sleeping.** If you try to cram too much information into the memory at one time, the brain will have problems filing it. Or, if other information flows in immediately after memorizing, it may replace what you just learned. Research suggests that material is best retained if you nap or sleep afterward.

- **Avoid mechanical or physical blocks when memorizing.** A mechanical block happens when you mishear, misunderstand or tune out the information. If you disagree with something in your presentation about your new home community, you might create a mechanical block that will hamper your ability to memorize. You will have to clear that up before it will register in your brain. A physical block may be the result of inadequate diet, illness, fatigue, anxiety or substance abuse.

- **Take a keen interest in the material you're memorizing.** Don't just go through the motions. As author and businessman Lee Iacocca said, "If you care, you remember."

- **Connect pleasant memories to memorizing.** Light candles. Play soft music. Eliminate distractions. Create an atmosphere that's conducive to relaxation.

- **Record the material on a tape recorder and play it back repeatedly.** You perceive the world through your five senses and through your cognitive ability. If you try to memorize information simply by thinking, there is an 83 percent chance that you'll forget it. If you allow your senses to participate in the memorization process, there is a greater chance you'll remember it. When you see the closing techniques written out and you repeat them out loud into a tape recorder, you are using two senses—sight and hearing. Therefore, you will

Tips from the Experts (*Continued*)

increase your chance of remembering the information. Plus you'll have the advantage of listening to the tape in the car, while you're exercising, dressing for work or reclining on your favorite chair.

■ **Schedule breaks between periods of memorization.** Don't try to memorize everything at one time. In order for the brain to avoid transferring every piece of information to memory and be overloaded, it uses what scientists call the spacing effect. Whenever the brain is presented with information to file, it is temporarily

sent to long-term memory, and eventually forgotten. However, when the brain is introduced to the same information later, it assumes there's a probability the information will be needed again so it increases the retention time. The next time you need to remember it, you'll be able to retrieve it easier. The more often you repeat the process, the longer your brain retains the information. Therefore, giving your brain time between periods of memorization actually improves your ability to recall.

Never Leave Home Without It

Always have your closing material with you. *Always.*

You must make it a priority to be ready to close anytime, anywhere. Contracts and business are to be concluded the moment the customer acknowledges acceptance of the terms. Keep your closing forms, calculator, pen, and all other pertinent material with you wherever and whenever you are with a prospect.

Remember, you have worked hard moving a prospect past his fear of making a mistake (buyer's remorse in advance). If there is an interim period while you gather all your materials, then self-doubt and fears have time to invade the prospect's mind and unravel the sale.

When you receive a commitment and decide to process the paperwork later, the client will likely develop additional concerns you will have to address. In some cases, you may even

When you receive a commitment and decide to process the paperwork later, the client will likely develop additional concerns you will have to address.

Preparation is Number One

Richard, an accomplished salesperson, rushed into the office, excited that he had landed a sale resulting in a $17,500 commission. I congratulated Richard and asked for the contracts and deposit check so that we could process the paperwork.

"Oh," he said, "I don't have them with me. As a matter of fact, I'm meeting the customer at the office in 30 minutes and we will prepare the contracts there."

Already guessing what his answer would be, I asked, "Why didn't you prepare the agreements when you were with him?"

"I didn't have contracts with me, but don't worry. They are solid. Besides, I would rather have the contracts typed."

I've experienced this scenario too many times but did not want to extinguish Richard's excitement by predicting the probable outcome. Within 10 minutes, Richard reappeared with the sullen look that required no explanation. The cus-tomer, now a prospect, had called with concerns. He would not be coming to the office and had decided to delay his decision. Richard would meet him later that day to give him support informa-tion to pass along to his accountant and attorney.

Richard never did finalize the sale. The prospect lost the opportunity to own a beach house that has increased in value every year. Instead, following the advice of his attorney and accountant, he invested in the stock market.

Although Richard lost the sale, he did gain something very valuable. Experience. A business associate defines experience as "what you get when you don't get what you want."

Richard wanted the sale and commis-sion. But he got the experience of learning what can happen when you're not prepared to close the sale.

have to start your presentation over again. As difficult as it is the first time around, the second time the prospect's emotional involvement won't be as intense and he will be a tougher sell.

Let Your Paper Do The Talking

This tip is from master salesperson and trainer Zig Ziglar. He suggests that you always carry a legal pad during your presentation. He calls it your "talking pad."

If you want to increase the power of your presentation and closing the sale by 22 times, then learn to talk on paper. There are 22 times more nerve endings from the eye to the brain than from the ear to the brain. Plus, as the experts point out, if prospects hear you say it and see it writ-ten, they will remember it better because they are using more of their senses.

In the vacation ownership industry, we had the saying, "Ink it, don't think it. Delegate to document." When delivering a presentation, we did a *pad talk* that had the highlights of the presentation written down for the prospects to review. This included key benefits, guarantees, warranties, and assurances.

"Ink it, don't think it. Delegate to document."

You can use your own talking pad to combine a verbal presentation with the power of the printed word. Don't, however, use your talking pad to itemize and calculate numbers. You can list the totals, but always use a calculator when figuring interest rates, mortgage payments, rate of return, etc. Your prospect will believe totals on the calculator are indisputable when you're doing the math in front of him. But if you scribble them out in longhand, he might not be so trusting.

Use the Talking Pad

Master salesperson and trainer Zig Ziglar suggests that you always carry a legal pad during your presentation. You can use your talking pad to combine a verbal presentation with the power of the printed word.

One final suggestion. To increase your closing effectiveness, always carry a legal binder containing your contracts, calculator, pen, and any other materials necessary to close. Then you won't share Richard's experience or his disappointment.

Develop a Question Mark for a Brain

Research conducted by author and Notre Dame professor Herb True, Ph.D., concluded that 46 percent of the people he interviewed would ask for the order only once before giving up; 24 percent ask twice before shying away; 14 percent ask for the order a third time; and 12 percent continue to ask one more time before throwing in the towel. The final tabulation has 96 percent of the professional salespeople he interviewed asking for the sale somewhere between one and four times before quitting.

What's startling is the same research indicates that 60 percent of all sales occur after the *fifth* attempt to ask for the order. The bottom line is

96 percent of the professional salespeople he interviewed asked for the sale somewhere between one and four times before quitting.

60 percent of all sales occur after the fifth attempt to ask for the order.

—Herb True, Ph.D.
Notre Dame professor

that the top four percent of salespeople who possess the courage and technical skills to ask for the order five or more times are making 60 percent of the sales and the commissions.

A Detroit newspaper reported Henry Ford had purchased a huge insurance policy. A friend of Mr. Ford's, who was also an insurance salesperson, was naturally upset and asked Ford why he did not buy from him.

Mr. Ford's answer holds the secret of sales success for anyone selling anything! He replied, "Because you didn't ask me."

If you are hesitant to ask a prospect to buy for fear of appearing like a hard sell, high-pressure salesperson, you need to get over it. After your presentation, asking for the order is your fundamental responsibility. So, ask. Ask enthusiastically. Ask confidently. And ask often.

Each time you do, it gives prospects an opportunity to take another look at what you're selling. You may know the story of the 3M engineer who had a terrible time trying to convince his bosses that a weaker adhesive he'd developed could be useful to the company. He asked repeatedly to show them the product. Finally, they consented and Post-It notes were born. Every time you see one, let it remind you of the importance of sticking to something.

Paralyzed by Fear?

Do you avoid asking for the sale because you're afraid the prospect will say No? Well, guess what. If it takes five times before the prospect finally says Yes, then you're right to expect a negative response—at least during the first few times you ask.

So, maybe it isn't the fear of rejection that paralyzes you. Maybe it's something else like the fear of being humiliated, of not being liked, of failing to make the sale, of approaching unpredictable prospects or of leaving your comfort zone and entering a new area of sales. You could probably add to the list, but why bother? The question to ask is, "Am I willing to give up my goal for this fear?"

The reality is that you can choose to close the sale immediately after your presentation or you can choose to wait. It's that simple.

Close Your Mouth to Close the Sale

Author and motivational speaker Brian Tracy says, "The only pressure you are allowed to use in a sales presentation is the pressure of silence after you have asked the closing question."

When you've asked the final question, it's critical that you become perfectly silent and wait for the answer. Sounds easy, doesn't it? It was a difficult discipline for me to master and is a challenge to convey to most new salespeople.

Why is it important to remain silent after asking a closing question? Because if you say something prior to receiving a response, you take the pressure off the prospect to answer your closing question. Whereas, if you remain silent, one of two things will occur. Either your prospect will answer the question and commit to buying a new home or your prospect will answer with an explanation as to why he or she won't buy today.

Either answer is acceptable. If the answer is Yes, you complete the paperwork. If the answer is No, you find out why. The prospect may offer an objection that you can easily address or a condition that prevents the sale. But either way, you have closure and won't be wondering "what if. . . ."

> *"The only pressure you are allowed to use in a sales presentation is the pressure of silence after you have asked the closing question."*
>
> —Brian Tracy,
> **Author and**
> **Motivational Speaker**

Exactly What is Closing?

To understand what closing is, let's discuss what closing is not.

Closing techniques are not tactics of the cunning used to manipulate people into purchasing homes they cannot use, can't afford, don't want or need.

Closing is a skill the professional salesperson practices and possesses to lead people to make decisions that benefit them. Closing techniques are designed to move decision-makers past moments of tension, indecision or fear.

When you have given a successful presentation and your prospects are qualified, you are helping them make a decision to purchase a beautiful new home that otherwise, they may not make without your assistance. So, don't be shy about asking them to buy.

CHAPTER 8

Hot Off the Press!
13 Ways to Get to "Yes!"

Closes

If it takes multiple times to close a sale on one new home, then you must be prepared to use multiple closing techniques.

Not long ago I received an e-mail from a salesperson who subscribes to my newsletter. Sarah was discouraged because it had been nearly three months since she'd made a sale. We corresponded back and forth for several days and I learned that she represented a new community that was affordable, filled with amenities, and in a convenient location.

When I asked her to tell me what happens when she gets ready to close the sale, she explained that she would ask the prospects a couple of times if they were ready to buy and, if they said No, she would tell them to think about it and she'd call them later in the week to see if they had changed their minds.

Asking for the commitment to buy was sometimes uncomfortable, she added, because she lives in a fairly small town and often knows the prospects. She explained that she doesn't want to appear pushy and risk offending them.

Since Sarah was so eager to do something to close more sales, I recommended that she quickly memorize all of the closing techniques and, depending upon which objections the prospects used, customize them to fit the situation and her personality.

"I'll try," she said.

About three weeks later, I heard from Sarah again. She said she had taken four days to learn and rehearse the 13 closing techniques I had sent her.

"I practiced them with my husband, who acted like he was shopping for a new home. I would deliver my presentation and he would tell me why he couldn't buy. He used every excuse he could think of so I could learn which closing to use," she e-mailed. "I returned to work like a new person. But what I really had was new confidence and a new outlook."

Within the following two weeks, Sarah lost only one sale and closed on four. "The couple who didn't buy couldn't qualify because they needed to sell their existing home first."

How Many Closing Strategies Should You Know?

When I conduct seminars and salespeople ask me how many closing techniques they should memorize, I tell them, "If you want to be a Superachiever, then you should memorize at least 20 closing strategies and techniques."

"Why so many?" they ask.

I tell them it's because every buying situation is different and each buyer is different. So, the closing techniques should be customer-ized to fit each prospect.

Throughout this book, you'll read about some of the most powerful and proven closing techniques available. If you, like Sarah, want to close more sales, you'll do what she did and learn them word for word before conforming them to fit your selling style.

In seminars I've conducted, I sometimes get resistance from salespeople when I suggest this because they are either intimidated by the concept of memorizing or they want to find an easier way to get their prospects to say Yes.

In case you're feeling the same way, here are the most frequent objections and my replies.

Some of the closing techniques will not work in my situation or some clash with my personality.

That's understandable, so use what's comfortable. But memorize them all because you'll find that, in locating your particular comfort zone, you'll use bits and pieces from different closes. Begin by memorizing those that are most suited to you and your circumstances.

These are not my words, yet you expect me to learn them word for word.

I jokingly tell seminar audiences, "Of course they are not your words. It's my name, not yours, appearing on the front cover of the book. I ask you to learn the techniques word for word first, and then, with time and practice, adapt your own language style."

It is a lot of work to memorize word for word.

I understand. I fought it, too. But consider this: Is your current method of selling working for you? Are you earning all the income you want or need? Are you happy with your closing ratio? Would you like to find a way that makes you a more professional, successful salesperson? This system has been proven to increase sales, confidence, and income. So, why not try it?

Perhaps you've heard this simple definition: Insanity is doing the same thing over and over, and expecting a different result. If you continue doing business in the same manner that you have been doing business, you can expect the same results. To achieve a different outcome and a higher income, you must make some changes. Are you willing to do that or do you want business as usual?

> *Insanity is doing the same thing over and over and expecting a different result. To achieve a different outcome and a higher income, you must make some changes.*

> *To achieve a different outcome and a higher income, you must make some changes.*

THESE CLOSES OPEN DOORS

1. Order Form Close

This is the fundamental closing technique. The first rule is to make certain you have your contracts and order forms with you always. If you work from your desk, display them. By keeping your paperwork in sight, prospects know you are not trying to hide anything. They also become accustomed to seeing them if they come to your office often. It's easier for you, also, to have the necessary paperwork handy when you're ready to close. If you are delivering your presentation away from your desk, have a binder or attaché case with your legal pad and contracts inside.

As you fill out the paperwork, you are not directly asking the prospect to buy, which in his mind, translates into making a verbal commitment. You are simply taking the initiative to make the final decision for him.

The best time to work with this close is at the beginning and during your presentation. My favorite time to begin the *Order Form Close* is when the prospect asks a question that indicates a buying signal. You answer the question with a question of your own and record the answer on the contract order form.

Prospect: "Is it possible to delay the closing date for 60 days?"
Superachiever: "Mr. Prospect, would an additional 30 days be more convenient?"

Prospect: "Yes. I'll need that time to secure additional funds."
Superachiever: "Let me make a note of that." Record the information on the contract.

NOTE: As long as the prospect does not stop you from recording the answers on the contract, he is buying. However, the prospect may say something like:

Prospect: "Is that a contract? You are ahead of yourself. I'm not buying anything."
Superachiever: "Of course, you're not. I would never expect you to own without all the facts. I use this form to write all the information down on. It has everything about the offer arranged in a precise manner, such as price, terms, options, delivery date—all the information you and I both need for your review purposes later. That's okay, isn't it?"

From the start of the presentation to the end, make notations of all his questions and record terms on the contract. By the end of the presentation, the contract is virtually complete and will only require a signature. Here's how this entire close is intended to work:

Prospect: "How much is the down payment?"
Superachiever: "Mr. Prospect, we would require an initial investment of either 10 or 20 percent. Which would you prefer?"

Prospect: "I'd like to get in for the least amount. I suppose 10 percent."
Superachiever: "Great. Let me make a note of that."

Prospect: "Is that a contract? You're getting ahead of yourself. I'm not ready to buy."
Superachiever: "Of course, you're not. I would never expect you to own without all the facts. This form has everything about the home arranged in a precise manner, such as price, terms, options, delivery date—all the information you and I both need for your review purposes later. That's okay, isn't it?"

Prospect: "Well, I guess that's okay."
Superachiever: "By the way, Mr. Prospect, we could schedule delivery of your new home in 120 days, if that fits into your timeframe."

Prospect: "Actually, I need to be moved out of my existing home in 90 days."
Superachiever: "I see, then I'm going to note that delivery must coordinate with the date of your move. Is that okay?"

Prospect: "Yes, that would work."
Superachiever: "Mr. Prospect, would this purchase be under your personal name or is someone else appearing on the deed?"

Prospect: "It will be in both my name and my wife's."
Superachiever: "Fine. And your middle initial is?"

Prospect: "It's T."
Superachiever: "What is the correct spelling of your mailing address?"

When you have asked all the questions and the contract is completed, review all the notes with the prospect. If he agrees with what you've recorded, ask him to authorize or okay the agreement.

2. I Want To Think About It Close

Sales trainer Tom Hopkins has his students memorize this technique word for word in his three-day boot camp sessions. I personally feel if you do not commit this one close to memory, you simply are not serious about the sales profession.

"I want to think about it" and "I want to think it over" are the most common objections a salesperson will encounter, regardless of the product offered. In the best of situations, under the most ideal conditions, you will hear these phrases at least 50 percent of the time. That's why it's imperative that you commit this close to memory right away.

The prospect says, "I want to think it over" for four reasons:

▎ **It's a brush off.** Swallow your ego and accept the fact that this prospect doesn't want what you're offering. Frequently, when you're told, "I want to think it over," it's because she is trying to be nice and send you on your way without hurting your feelings. Some salespeople believe the prospect actually wakes up in the morning and goes to bed at night thinking about their offer. But, in reality, when the salesperson calls back two or three days later sure of a sale, the prospect may not even remember him.

▎ **The prospect is experiencing buyer's remorse in advance.** This occurs when you are working with a prospect who is genuinely interested in buying a new home. At the moment of closing, he experiences tension, which could result from a fear of making a mistake, of choosing the wrong floor plan, of paying too much or of being criticized by friends. These fears cause him to back away at the moment of closing and say, "I want to think about it."

▎ **The prospect is stalling.** The good news is that the prospect has some desire for your new home; the bad news is that something is stopping her from making a decision to buy right now. A stall means that she has some conflict going on internally. She is interested in the new home but something is interfering with the urgency to buy it. You must flush out the objection or condition and rebuild the prospect's emotional desire to own by stressing the benefits of buying a new home in your community.

▎ **There's a concern about financial resources.** He says he wants to think about it because the price or terms of the home or homesite are concerning him. Usually, the prospect wants to think about it because he doubts his ability to buy.

The problem with "I want to think about it" is that it's a broad statement and not narrowed to any one specific concern. Prospects aren't usually bold enough to say, "I want to think about it because I'm not sure I can afford to buy this home," or "I think I might regret making this decision." So, that leaves you down to the final objection and nothing concrete on which to reply.

If you follow this script, you should be able to tread past the Valley of Vague Generality into the Land of the Final Objection.

Prospect: "I need to think it over."
Superachiever: "That's fine. Obviously you would not take the time to think about it unless you were genuinely interested, would you?"

Remain silent and wait for his reply. This question confirms he is genuinely interested.

Prospect: "Oh, yeah, I'm definitely interested."
Superachiever: "Great! Since you are interested, I can assume you will give this careful consideration, won't you?"

Remain silent and wait for the reply. If he says Yes, it confirms he will actually think about it.

Prospect: "Yes, I definitely will be giving it the consideration it deserves."
Superachiever: "Outstanding! Just to clarify my thinking, what phase of the offer is it you will be considering? Is it the area?"

Prospect: "No, the location is perfect."
Superachiever: "Is it the neighborhood?"

Prospect: "No. We love the neighborhood."
Superachiever: "Mr. Prospect, I sense your hesitation. Do you mind my asking if it ha something to do with the money?"

In all likelihood, if you have come this far with him and he is genuinely interested in buying, it will be a money issue. If this is the case, use the *Money Close* to find out what financial area is troubling him.

"I'll Think About It."

Most prospects do not think about your offer after they leave. They do not review your literature and product information. What they do is to move on with their lives. According to statistics, 95 percent of the prospects who say they'll "think it over" walk away without buying and don't return. About 50 percent of them will actually shop around in other communities. Therefore, the time to nail down the sale is at the end of your presentation when you have identified their needs and clearly presented your new homes and neighborhood as the solution.

Try the following techniques when you are working with people who have positions of authority:

Prospect: "I want to think it over."
Superachiever: "Mary, I'm sure a person in your position makes major decisions daily. You've made larger decisions than this before, haven't you? Isn't this relatively small in comparison to the decisions you have made in the past? Let's go forward with the decision now. I'll handle the details for you, and you're free to focus on the important issues of your business. That makes sense, doesn't it?"

Prospect: "I still need to think about it."
Superachiever: "You impress me as a proactive decision maker. Why don't you and I take the bull by the horns to reach a decision right now?"

Prospect: "I still want to think about it."
Superachiever: "Why invest more time thinking this over? You have told me that you are satisfied with the new home, its location, and the community. And it's within the parameters of your budget. Haven't you thought about it already?"

Prospect: "I need to take more time to think this over."
Superachiever: "I understand. Let's think out loud together. Share your reasons with me for not wanting to proceed forward."

Remember the critical instruction. After you ask a closing question, remain perfectly silent and allow your prospect enough time to answer.

3. Invitational Close

This close is the first closing technique I learned primarily because of its simplicity. Yet, through the years, it has become one of my favorite ways to ask for a commitment.

The question I ask with the *Invitational Close* is: "Why don't you take it?" This is a delicate, yet powerful way to gently nudge your prospect toward ownership.

You can use this close to conclude the sale either at the end or during your presentation. It will be preceded by a *Trial Close* such as, "Ms. Prospect, how do you like it?" or "Ms. Prospect, do you have any further questions?"

Superachiever: "Ms. Prospect, how do you like the homesite?"
Prospect: "I do like it."
Superachiever: "Great! Why don't you take it?"

Inviting the prospect to make a buying decision is a low-key method that bridges to the decision to own. After demonstrating your new home or showing a homesite ask:

> **Superachiever:** "Bill, Mary, how do you like the home/homesite?"
> **Prospects:** "We absolutely love it."
> **Superachiever:** "Great! Why don't you take it?"

When you say this, one of two things will occur. The prospects will either answer "Yes, I'll take it" and you'll congratulate them and move rapidly to the *Order Form Close* to complete the contracts. Or they'll say "No, I don't think we'll take it today." Then you ask, "Why not?" The prospects will explain to you what they are looking for and, in doing so, have exposed their "hot button."

4. Hot Button Close

The *Hot Button Close* is founded on the 80/20 rule that states, "80 percent of all results come from 20 percent of the energy expended."

20 percent of the salespeople make 80 percent of the sales.

In the sales profession, 20 percent of the salespeople make 80 percent of the sales. The remaining members of the team share a meager 20 percent of the sales volume.

Because this is an irrefutable fact in all sales organizations, I advise sales managers to maximize their results by investing 80 percent of their time with the top 20-percent producers.

The 80/20 rule in selling new homes is based on the fact that 80 percent of the buying decision will be based on 20 percent of the home's features. Therefore, if you have 20 special amenities, your job is to find the one or two that offers the largest benefits to each particular prospect. Those will become their hot buttons that you'll press over and over again.

80 percent of the buying decision will be based on 20 percent of the home's features.

This close is effective because it lets the prospect know what's in it for him or her.

Customers buy new homes for their own reasons, not yours. With the *Hot Button Close,* you are able to lock in on what those reasons are. Every time you speak of your new homes in terms of the prospect's hot button, you are speaking his language and igniting his enthusiasm. On the other hand, when you talk about things that are of no interest to him, his buying desire dissipates.

A hot-button selling feature is a senior-friendly home. As Baby Boomers age, they are searching for homes that accommodate their changing lifestyle. Surveys taken indicate that the Boomers want homes

The Story of the Beautiful Flowering Cherry Tree: An Example of Hot-Button Selling

A real estate professional showed an older home in need of some repair to a young couple. Upon arriving, they see a beautiful flowering cherry tree in the front yard. The wife, Linda, said to her husband, "Look Tom, a beautiful flowering cherry tree. When I was a young girl, my family home had a beautiful cherry tree like that. I've always dreamed our home would have one, too."

Ignoring her comments, Tom nudged his wife and said, "Let me handle this. I'll do the talking."

But it was too late. The perceptive salesperson had identified the prospect's hot button and made a mental note.

Playing the reluctant buyer, Tom said, "The deck needs immediate repair." The salesperson agrees, "Yes, but from your deck, you would always enjoy the view of the beautiful flowering cherry tree."

As they toured the house, Tom pointed out problem areas. "The carpet needs to be replaced and the house needs to be painted," he said.

The salesperson nodded, looked at the wife and said, "You're right, but did you notice this lovely bay window? If you look out of it across the lawn you have a glorious view of the beautiful flowering cherry tree."

Upon seeing the master bedroom, Tom objected, "The bedroom is small and the bathroom needs new fixtures."

"Yes, but look outside. Every morning you can wake up and have a perfect view of the beautiful flowering cherry tree," said the salesman.

At the end of the showing, Linda, who loved the beautiful flowering cherry tree, convinced her husband to buy the home. She was sold on the flowering cherry tree and the pleasant memories it represented. For her, the home was a bonus.

The cherry tree was the hot button and the emotional key that was pushed repeatedly by the salesperson. Did he use it to manipulate the couple to make a purchase? Not at all. They bought the home for their own reasons. The salesman just reminded them of what those reasons were.

that are energy efficient, low maintenance, and easily accessible for those with physical limitations.

Their hot buttons might be an open floorplan with the main living areas on one floor, easy-to-operate windows, task lighting, low-step entrances, non-slip flooring, wide doorways, grab bars in bathrooms and an alarm system.

If you question skillfully and listen intently, they will tell you exactly what will make them want to purchase your new homes. Not only will they tell you that, but they'll also tell you why they *won't* buy from you.

5. Assumptive Close

All top sales professionals are assumptive closers. From the beginning of the presentation to the end, they confidently *assume* the buyer will own even before they have received confirmation or acknowledgment that a buying decision has been reached.

The *Assumptive Close* is sometimes referred to as the *Next Step Close*. Have you ever been in the middle of your presentation and the prospect says, "What's the next step?"

When that happens, swing into the *Assumptive Close* and wrap up the details with the *Order Form Close*.

> **Prospect:** What's the next step?
> **Superachiever:** "Mr. and Mrs. Prospect, I'm glad you asked. The next step is for you to authorize the agreements and I will need a check for $5,000 as the deposit on your new homesite."

If the prospect does not ask what the next step is, then initiate the *Assumptive Close* at the end of your sales presentation by first issuing a *Trial Close*.

> **Superachiever:** "Mr. and Mrs. Prospect, do you have any additional questions before we begin the paperwork?"
> **Prospects:** "No."
> **Superachiever:** "Great. Then I need you to authorize the agreements and write a check for $5,000 as a deposit on your brand new home."

Now you begin processing the contracts. If, for any reason the prospect does say, "Yes, I have

To be an assumptive closer, you must make the sale in your own mind before it's concluded in the prospect's mind.

Pay the Price to Learn the Profession

Josh was a novice new home salesperson. Although he had no previous experience in sales, the sales manager hired him anyway because of his enthusiasm and willingness to pay the price to learn the profession.

About three weeks into the job, Josh was in the model home with his sales manager and a seasoned but complacent Realtor® named Rob. When an older couple walked in to get information on buying a new home, Rob immediately walked over, introduced himself, and launched into a grocery-list of rehearsed reasons why they should buy that particular home.

When he finished, the man looked at his wife then turned back to Rob and said, "It's a beautiful home, but it isn't exactly what we want."

As they turned to leave the model, Josh walked over, introduced himself, and began asking the couple what they were looking for in a new home. Reluctantly, they mentioned a few things—lots of kitchen counters, storage space, an abundance of windows, a downstairs master bedroom, and laundry room.

Josh fixed his eyes on the couple and asked if they had just a few more minutes to spare so he could show them some special features that might interest them. Although he had only been selling real estate for less than a month, Josh was totally sold on the homes himself and loved having the opportunity to show them to others. The challenge, however, was to put aside his own perspective and view the home through the eyes of his prospects.

Enthusiastically, he walked the couple through the house, rubbing his hand across the solid surface countertops while explaining how the kitchen was designed for entertaining. He pointed out the spacious bathrooms and the abundance of shelved closet space. He showed them how the house could be slightly altered so that a master bedroom could be added to the first floor.

During the demonstration, Josh spoke as though the couple already owned it and he encouraged them to envision themselves enjoying it.

About 30 minutes later, they all sat down at his desk. Josh completed the contract and sold them the home.

As the couple was leaving, the sales manager approached them and asked why they chose to buy from Josh.

The husband thought for a moment, and then said, "Well, the other salesman knew all about the house, but Josh wanted to know all about us. When we walked through, he showed us how this home met our needs. And when we finished, he asked if we had any more questions before signing the contract. We didn't. So, we signed."

Josh did several things that were in his favor:

- He had enthusiasm.
- He asked questions to learn what the prospects wanted to buy.
- He described how the home's features benefited the prospects.
- He used imagery to demonstrate how the prospects would feel owning the new home.
- He was so confident they would buy that he immediately began the paperwork once the demonstration was complete.

more questions," then you patiently and thoroughly answer them and then ask them to authorize the contracts again.

To be an assumptive closer, you must make the sale in your own mind before it's concluded in the prospect's mind. The power is in the psychological principle that your assumptive attitude creates the prospect's desire for your product. The more positive you are that the sale is inevitable, the greater the probability the prospect will own.

Assumptive Closes to Memorize

Superachiever: "Mr. Prospect, prior to our meeting, I took the liberty to prepare the paperwork. All that is needed is for you to authorize the agreements."
Superachiever: "We seem to be in agreement on all the major points. The initial investment is only $5,000. Would you be taking care of that with a personal check?"

Assumptive Handshake Close
(A Variation on the Assumptive Close)

The implication in this close is that a handshake represents a person's word and psychologically bonds an agreement.

Larry, a super salesperson, concluded an expensive vacation home transaction with a handshake. At the end of the presentation, after covering countless objections, the husband looked to his wife and said, "What do you think?"

The chances were high the wife could have responded with, "I think we should think it over." Before they could reply, however, Larry looked at them both and offered his assurances. "I think you have made a wise decision. Congratulations." He then shook hands with the husband and the wife and closed on the sale.

It's important to note that the buyers were qualified, their needs determined, and the solution presented. Yet, as in most cases, there was hesitancy when it got down to signing on the bottom line. The moment of tension was relieved and the sale concluded by the *Assumptive Handshake Close.*

6. Alternatives Close

This close automatically concludes the sale by offering the prospect two or more alternatives. She has a choice between *something and something* rather than a choice between *something and nothing.*

Let me illustrate with this example. While visiting a friend, her four-year-old granddaughter climbed up in her lap and, with a matter-of-fact tone of voice, said, "Do you want to read me a book or play Mr. Kitty?"

Without being the least bit aware of it, the child was using the *Alternatives Close* to get something she wanted. Even at her young age, she had figured out that presenting her grandmother with two options was better than saying, "Grandma, would you read me a book?" That question could easily be answered with, "No. Not right now. I'm resting." By giving grandma two choices, the child knew that either one she selected would make her happy.

In sales, you wouldn't ask the prospect, "Do you want this new home or not?" Because the knee-jerk answer will probably be No. But you will get an affirmative response if you say, "Do you prefer model A or model B?"

I was consulting with a large real estate development company that was having some difficulty marketing and selling its homesites.

The community was lovely—bordered by a forest, adjacent to a golf course and splattered with small ponds. Prospects naturally wanted the prime homesites on the golf course and adjacent to the woods and ponds.

The problem was that the majority of the homesites were inland. Sales were going slow because potential buyers would be sold on the premium sites and then find out they didn't qualify. At that point, purchasing an inland homesite was a disappointment.

I suggested that the sales team first qualify the prospects before showing the homesites and, if they could afford only the inland homesites, use the *Alternatives Close* by saying, "Mr. and Mrs. Prospect, you qualify for several of our inland homesites, but I would recommend either the one on the cul-de-sac or the one near the clubhouse. Which one would you prefer?"

Depending upon the circumstances, there are several ways to present an *Alternatives Close.* Here are some suggestions:

Delivery: "Closing on your new homesite will occur in 30 or 60 days. Which would you prefer?"
Finances: "The initial investment can be secured by cash or personal check. Which would you prefer?"
Included or added features: "Which do you feel would best compliment your new kitchen—the oak or maple cabinets?"
Appointments: "I have either Monday or Wednesday available for this week. What works better for you? How about 10 a.m. or noon for lunch?"

Learn to offer two choices to your prospects. After they make their selection, implement the *Order Form Close.*

7. Trial Close

The *Trial Close* is like a barometer. You use it to evaluate the climate of the sale at any particular moment.

Is the air charged with excitement? Is the prospect hot to buy or cooling off? Are you experiencing a slight chill or can you imagine hearing thunderous applause? Are there storm clouds brewing or is everything bright and sunny?

Implement the *Trial Close* to determine where you are with your prospect during the presentation. Unlike a close that concludes the transaction, a *Trial Close* does not solicit a deposit or an order to buy. It merely allows you to seek the prospect's opinion regarding her willingness to buy. You throw it out at different times during the presentation to test the waters and judge the prospect's readiness to close on a new home.

Here are examples of the *Trial Close:*

Superachiever: "Well, Ms. Prospect, how are we doing so far?"
(or) "Is this what you had in mind?"
(or) "Is this what you are looking for?"
(or) "Does this make sense to you?"

The benefit of the *Trial Close* is that the prospect can answer Yes or No. Because you are merely "checking the climate," you don't end the presentation.

Trial Closes to Memorize

Superachiever: "Mr. and Mrs. Prospect, is this what you are looking for?" If they say no, you say, "Fine. What are you looking for?"

The exchange of information is like traveling down a winding road. You ask, "Does this make sense to you?" They confirm and you move to the next bend in the road. When you arrive, you ask, "Do you like the colors?" Then you move to the next bend. "Is this what you like?" you wonder. After a few more turns, you reach the end of the road.

_____

Superachiever: "I get the impression you are excited about the opportunity presented? Is that correct?"
Prospect: "Oh, we certainly are."

Superachiever: "Mr. and Mrs. Prospect, on a scale of 1 to 10—with 1 meaning that owning may not make complete sense yet and 10 meaning it makes perfect sense—where are you?"
Prospect: "I guess we're at a 7."
Superachiever: "Great! What additional information will you need to help you get to a 10?"

————————

Superachiever: "Now that I have demonstrated the features and benefits of our new homes, how do they compare with what you've seen elsewhere?"

————————

Superachiever: "Mr. Prospect, why is it you want to own in this community?"

————————

Superachiever: "After playing our golf course and seeing how much your family enjoys the neighborhood amenities, wouldn't you agree that it's unnecessary to even consider owning anywhere else?"

8. Ben Franklin Close

Shhh. I'm receiving your thoughts and they are, "The Ben Franklin Close? Where's this guy coming from? That close is as old as the hills and maybe he is, too. Even my grandfather knew this one."

I can't dispute that. Well, actually, I can. I'm not as old as dirt and I don't know about everyone's grandfather but this close has been around a long time. It probably goes back to . . . well . . . Ben Franklin. But just because everybody from one generation to the next is familiar with it, doesn't nullify the fact that it's still *the* most powerful close associated with the sales profession.

The *Ben Franklin Close* parallels how we process information and think. Whenever we are faced with a decision, we run through a checks-and-balance system to weigh the pros and cons of the decision. We look for a reason to do something or not to do it.

What does this have to do with our colonial statesman and inventor? Ben Franklin, America's first self-made millionaire, had a strategy for making fast decisions. He would take a piece of paper and draw a line down the center. On one side he wrote all the reasons favoring the decision and on the other side he wrote his reasons for opposing it. Then, he would base his decision upon whichever side had the most reasons.

In closing a sale with indecisive prospects, you can follow the same procedure.

Superachiever: "Mr. and Mrs. Prospect, I can sense you are having difficulty with this decision, aren't you? (Silence, wait for reply). The last thing I want is for you to make a choice that might be uncomfortable. So, may I make a suggestion? Let's use a systematic decision-making method. On one side of my legal pad we will list the reasons favoring a positive decision, and on the other side we'll list your concerns. Afterward, we'll see if it makes sense to you."

Take your pen and paper and fill out all the reasons for owning. You should be able to help them with this by coming up with countless reasons they should buy one of the new homes you're selling. Then make a *Summary Close* restating all the positive reasons for owning. After you're done, tell your prospects, "It certainly seems as if there are a number of good reasons for going forward, doesn't it?"

Wait for a reply before handing them the pen and paper and saying, "Now that we've listed all the reasons to purchase, can you think of reasons not to go ahead?"

Remain perfectly silent and let them work on the list by themselves. Most of the time, they will not be able to list more than three to four reasons.

From here, go to the *Assumptive Close* by saying, "Looks like you have made the right decision." (or) "It seems pretty obvious, doesn't it?" Then progress to the *Order Form Close.*

The *Ben Franklin Close* should not be limited to the end of your presentation. In my real estate development business, the home-building division was highly competitive. When prospects suggested they were considering the services of another builder, I asked two questions that triggered a *Ben Franklin Close.*

Superachiever: "Mr. and Mrs. Prospect, builder XYZ does a fine job. But I'm curious. Can you tell me what services and features he offers that cause you to want to do business with him? Are there any reasons or concerns that would cause you not to have him construct your dream home?"

The first purpose for asking the questions is to identify their hot buttons, exactly what they are looking for in a builder. The second purpose is to identify the inverse hot buttons. These are the reasons they would not want to use a particular builder. From this, develop the presentation, know which hot buttons to press, and effectively address their concerns.

The *Ben Franklin Close* is a magnificent way to move prospects past their indecision and satisfy even the most analytical person.

9. Puppy Dog Close

A parent and her children unexpectedly walk into the pet store just to look at the puppy dog they see in the window. But the children want to do more than look and begin chanting, "We want the puppy dog! We want the puppy dog!"

The pet store owner takes the dog from the display window and hands it to the mother. Immediately, the parent and children become emotionally involved with a purchase decision that they probably had not even considered before walking into the store.

The children persist with, "Please Mommy, can't we have the puppy dog? We'll take care of it. Can't we take it home with us?"

The storeowner senses her apprehension and then issues the *Invitational Close*. "This is a major decision, so why don't you just give it a try? Take the puppy home for a few days and play with him! If you don't feel comfortable, just bring him back."

The parent reluctantly agrees, thinking there's no obligation to buy and they'll bring it back in a couple of days after the kids discover they really don't want the responsibility of a dog.

But what happens? The puppy dog takes on an identity and is given a name. It looks up with those soft brown eyes and cuddles in everyone's lap. The kids are enamored. The parents are smitten. Suddenly, that cute little puppy dog has wiggled its way into the family.

This is an inventive way to get potential buyers involved in making a decision to purchase. It's so effective, some of the most successful neighborhoods in the world are using this type of strategy. Naturally, they know you can't physically take a home *home*, but they do take you out to the property, allow you to walk through the model, see the décor, inhale that new-home smell, touch the wallpaper and get emotionally involved. Then, when you leave, you carry a mental remnant with you to re-experience again and again.

Of course, visuals of homes from around the world can come into your home via the Internet. Virtual home tours allow you to feel as though you have the home inside your house. And, like with the puppy dog, family members can share the experience.

Regardless of how it's done, getting the product into the hands of the purchaser pays dividends. It's the try-it-you'll-like-it ploy. The concept is even taught to children. In fact, an entire book was written around this one premise.

Dr. Seuss' *Green Eggs and Ham* has a storyline in which the persistent Sam-I-am tries to get his friend to taste green eggs and ham. His friend is certain he does not like green eggs and ham, although he has never tasted it.

After emphatically claiming that he would not like them in the rain, on a train, in a box, with a fox, in a house or with a mouse, the friend finally shouts, "I do not like green eggs and ham! I do not like them Sam-I-am!"

To which steadfast Sam replies, "You do not like them. So you say. Try them! Try them! And you may." As you probably know, the friend tries them and, to his surprise, he actually likes green eggs and ham. Sam was a good salesman.

What do puppy dogs and green eggs have in common with new homes? Because a sale is emotional, you must let potential buyers see, touch, feel, smell and hear the benefits of buying a new home.

The *Puppy Dog Close* is appealing to salespeople because prospects end up selling themselves after they try it and like it.

See, Touch, and Feel the Benefits

Shirley recently received a call from the representative of a national hotel chain thanking her for staying in the hotel chain in Georgia. To show their gratitude, they were extending her an opportunity to stay at one of the new hotels in Myrtle Beach, SC, for two nights and three days for $99. This also included a $25 meal voucher, $30 cash and a $100 certificate that could be used for overnight accommodations at any of their hotels anywhere, anytime. There was one stipulation. To receive the cash and $100 certificate, she had to take a 90-minute tour of their new resorts. This special vacation offer was a way to get her to try their new resort condominiums with the hope that she would buy into the idea of vacation ownership.

10. Sharp Angle Close

The *Sharp Angle Close* is sometimes referred to as the *If I could, would you? Close*. It is a superb maneuver that works well with most types of objections. Whatever concerns the prospect expresses, you simply sharp angle the objection and send it back to the prospect with: "If I could, would you?"

Here's how it goes:

Prospect: "I don't know if I can afford it."
Superachiever: "Mr. Prospect, if I could arrange convenient financial terms to make this possible, would you proceed forward?"

The *Sharp Angle Close* is a perfect technique for handling smoke-screen objections. It helps you unearth the hidden objection.

The Puppy Dog Close works because prospects end up selling themselves after they try it and like it.

Prospect: "I don't know if I can afford it."
Superachiever: "Mr. Prospect, if I could arrange convenient financial terms to make this possible, would you proceed forward?"
Prospect: "Is that possible?"

NOTE: The average salesperson would be tempted to jump in and answer Yes. The Superachiever, however, uses the opportunity to make certain she's handled the final objection and is not so quick to answer.

Superachiever: I can't be certain until we process a loan application. I have one, which will only take a moment to complete, and we can make the sale subject to financial approval. That makes sense, doesn't it?"
Prospect: "I don't know. I probably need to think about it."
Superachiever: "Mr. Prospect, I sense your hesitancy. In addition to the financial arrangements, is there something else that prohibits you from becoming a new homeowner?"
Prospect: "Well, I just want to be certain I can include the additional features and landscaping as I've specified."

The Superachiever now issues a second *Sharp Angle Close*.

Superachiever: "Mr. Prospect, I understand your concerns. In addition to the terms, if I could offer full written warranty assurances, would you proceed today?"
Prospect: "Well, under those terms, it seems reasonable."

The Superachiever now begins to conclude the sale by assumptively employing three additional closing techniques, the *Assumptive Handshake Close*, the *Order Form Close*, and the *Alternatives Close*.

Superachiever: "Congratulations Mr. Prospect you've made a wise decision." (*Assumptive Handshake Close*)
Prospect: "Thank you."
Superachiever: "The next step is to simply prepare the paperwork.

May I have the correct spelling of your full name?" (*Order Form Close*)
Prospect: "John A. Smith."
Superachiever: "Mr. Smith, about the initial investment, will you be handling the deposit with cash or personal check?" (*Alternatives Close*)
Prospect: "Credit card."

Pancake Closes

Closes are often stacked on top of one another like pancakes. It's important to realize that you may begin with one close, like the Sharp Angle Close, but jump to others in rapid succession before concluding the sale. That's why it's mandatory that you memorize multiple closing techniques.

In reviewing the scenario in the Sharp Angle Close, you'll notice that the prospect was never directly asked to buy but was led into making the decision with a series of closing questions. It went like this:

1. *I can't afford it.*
   Sharp Angle—If I could, would you proceed today?
2. *How can I be certain I'll get the features and landscaping I want?*
   Sharp Angle—If I could would you go forward today?
3. *I need to think about it.*
   Think About It Close—In addition to that is there anything else?
4. **Assumptive Handshake Close**—Congratulations and assurances.
5. **Order Form Close**—Assumptively closing.
6. **Alternatives Close**—Asking for the money—cash, check or credit card.

As you can see, many techniques were employed before the prospect was comfortable making the final decision to buy that new home. Observe also that it took several attempts to close the sale. (Remember the statistics showing that the average sale is concluded after the fifth attempt?)

11. Minor Point Close

This close, often referred to as the *Secondary Close*, is based on the premise that it's easier to have the customer make smaller decisions first than to ask for a major commitment to buy that new home or homesite. That way, the prospect becomes accustomed to saying yes before you get to the home buying decision.

Here are some examples:

Superachiever: "Would you like to have country white cabinets in the kitchen to match the gingham curtains your grandmother made?"

Prospect: "Yes, that would be nice."
Superachiever: "We have several shades of carpeting that would complement your new home. Would you like to see what is available?"
Prospect: "Yes, please."

12. Yes Momentum Close

This great close consists of asking your prospects questions that lead them to answer Yes. Superachievers know that, if their prospects get into a mental pattern of saying Yes from the beginning of their presentation, it will become difficult for them to say No at the moment of closing.

The goal of the *Yes Momentum Close* is to create an atmosphere of agreement. To do this, you first need to tie down the close by asking questions at the beginning or at the end of a sentence that demands a Yes answer. Doing this psychologically ties your prospect into a "Yes" agreement.

Whenever you state anything about your company, neighborhood or service, the prospect has a tendency to disbelieve you. So, it's your job to present your offer in the best light. Author and motivator Tom Hopkins says, "If you say it, they doubt it. If they say it, it's true."

> *"If you say it, they doubt it. If they say it, it's true."*
>
> —Tom Hopkins, Author and Motivator

Using tie-down words in your presentation causes the prospect to verbally agree with your statements and to respond with similar observations.

Tie-Down Words

Doesn't it	Wasn't it	Wouldn't it	Won't you
Hasn't she	Aren't they	Can't you	Isn't it
Isn't that right	Couldn't it	Aren't you	Haven't they
Won't they	Shouldn't it	Don't you agree	Didn't it

Types of Tie-Downs

Deductive Tie-Downs are the most common and are used at the end of a sentence to demand Yes.

Superachiever: "It's a tremendous value, wouldn't you agree?"
Prospect: "Yes."

Inverted Tie-Downs occur at the beginning of a sentence. They are less demanding and lead a prospect to say Yes.

> **Superachiever:** "Isn't it exactly what you have in mind?"
> **Prospect:** "Yes."

Internal Tie-Downs are used in the middle of your statements of fact.

> **Superachiever:** "Mr. & Mrs. Prospect, as we stand here on the deck, can't you imagine how you and your family will enjoy this new home for years to come?"
> **Prospects:** "Yes."

Tag-on Tie-Downs: Whenever your prospect offers positive statements, add a tie-down in your response that bolsters value.

> **Prospect:** "The views are absolutely incredible!"
> **Superachiever:** "Aren't they? Can you imagine what it looks like at sunset?"

Start your presentation and conversation positively. Lead your prospects in agreement beginning with your greeting, "Welcome! Thank you for the opportunity to meet. It's a great day, isn't it?" Building numerous small agreements from the beginning of your presentation to the end will get you to the final positive close. And, as you'll ask your prospects, "This is what you want, isn't it?"

Examples of Tie-Downs

"Isn't this what you have always dreamed of owning?"

"It's a sound investment, wouldn't you agree?"

"Don't you agree, this is exactly what your specifications call for?"

"You are excited now, aren't you?"

"Based on what we have shared, it fits your needs perfectly, doesn't it?"

13. Referral Prospecting Close

There are only two ways you can increase your business. Either find new prospects daily or obtain more business from your existing customer base.

The easiest and most effective method of obtaining new prospects is to gather referrals. Why is a referral so much more powerful than a cold

The easiest and most effective method of obtaining new prospects is to gather referrals.

call? Because it makes you more credible. Remember, there are three factors the prospect considers during the sales process. First is you as the salesperson; second is your company; and third is your community. If you obtain a refer-ral from a satisfied customer, your credibility is already established.

Another reason to request referrals is that like-minded people usually associate with one another. This is referred to as the "nest factor," which means "birds of a feather flock together."

If your customer is qualified to own, it's likely he's associating with other qualified buyers.

The optimum time to obtain referrals is either immediately after the purchase of the new home/homesite or at the time of delivery. And the key to obtaining referrals is this: No one volunteers referrals. You must ask for them.

> **Superachiever:** "Mr. and Mrs. Prospect, I have a favor to ask you."
> **Customers:** "Sure, what is it?"
> **Superachiever:** "In my business, my most valued resource is the customer. My top priority is knowing you are satisfied. You are satis-fied and comfortable with your new home, aren't you?"
> **Customers:** "We certainly are."
> **Superachiever:** "Then, the favor I ask is this: I would like to share the same opportunity to buy a new home with your friends or rela-tives. Do two to three people come to your mind whom you would like to have a neighbors?"

After you obtain the names, ask for the phone numbers and if the customer is extremely comfortable with you, ask that he call ahead to introduce you, your company and services.

Another method for referral prospecting comes from a friend of mine in the insurance business. This is how he asks for referrals:

> **Superachiever:** "Mr. Customer, if your best friends were present right now, would you introduce us to one another?"
> **Customer:** "Certainly, I'd be glad to."
> **Superachiever:** "Mr. Customer, that's exactly what I'd like to ask you to do. Would you mind if I called to introduce myself and my service to two or three of your best friends?"

There is one final method to the *Referral Prospecting Close* and that is to obtain prospects from people who did not buy. Julie, an outstanding salesperson, always asks for referrals from non-buyers in the following fashion:

> **Julie:** "Mr. Prospect, I understand the timing is not right to own now (or I understand you are not in a position to become involved, or I understand you are not in a position to decide today), but could you give me the names of two or three people you think may be able to take advantage of this opportunity?"

Remember, you earn referrals by excellent service. If you have followed through and satisfied the customer with good service and positive results, you have earned the right to ask for referrals.

The Five-to-Seven Rule

The five-to-seven rule is true in advertising as well. That's the average amount of times a person must see a commercial or an ad before she makes a decision on buying the product. It seems to take the brain that many repetitions before the message hits home.

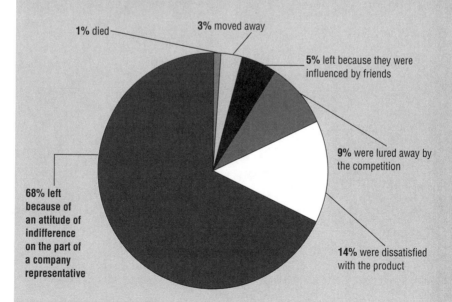

1% died

3% moved away

5% left because they were influenced by friends

9% were lured away by the competition

68% left because of an attitude of indifference on the part of a company representative

14% were dissatisfied with the product

CHAPTER 9

Everything Has a Price.
I Just Want Yours to be Low

It is a misconception that customers are only concerned with the lowest price. If it were true, companies selling high-priced, luxury items would not survive. And what good is a salesperson if customers purchased only the cheapest items?

All we would need is a press-and-buy telephone system that allows customers to place their orders electronically. A builder's message might sound like this: "Hello. Thank you for calling Economy Builders, where our motto is, 'Why shop around? We're the lowest in town.' Today our cheapest model is the three-bedroom, one-bath Tightwad II priced at a mere $129,000.

"It comes complete with basic white appliances, pressboard kitchen cabinetry, monotone beige carpeting, and a carport. There are identical light fixtures throughout with three choice settings: dim, flicker, and out.

"In order to save you the most money, we put very little time into designing and furnishing this model. We chose the cheapest materials we could to still pass the building codes. To save on over-head, we used street labor to build it and purchased second-hand bathroom fixtures. We have eliminated the warranties, since your main concern is price and they wouldn't be a selling point anyway.

"This model does have the ever popular cookie-cutter floor plan, which makes it easy to locate the bathroom when you're visiting neighbors. To purchase the Tightwad II, press one. To ask a question, press two and you'll be transferred to voice mail. We keep our expenses to a minimum, so we have no office personnel to answer your call but the owner does come in a few times a week to check on the guard dogs. Thanks again for calling and have a penny-pinching day."

Although it may seem as though price is a customer's primary consideration, it really isn't. The average home buyer does have other things on her mind.

Nevertheless, it is still frustrating to repeatedly hear "How much is it?" at the beginning of the presentation. It's just as bad as hearing "It costs too much," "It's more than I expected," "I can't afford it," "Your competition is cheaper," or the classic, "I'll be back," at the end of the presentation.

Many prospects will want to know how much your new homes/homesites cost early in your presentation. Unfortunately, once they know, they complain.

As with the other objections, price concerns are predictable. When you comprehend that price resistance is a natural, predictable objection, you can plan your strategy to deal with it.

The Basics of Price Resistance

It always costs too much. A price objection is an automatic response. Everybody asks how much it is and then flinches at the price. Nearly every consumer becomes intoxicated with the idea of obtaining the best value possible. However, no matter what the cost, the initial reaction is usually "it's more than we expected to pay."

Price is the common denominator. Why does price come up early in the sales presentation? Because it represents something we all have in common and that is a concern with money. Therefore, it makes sense to focus on dollars and cents.

Is price their objection or yours? Is the price objection on your mind first? If you are uncomfortable with the prices of your new homes, then you'll have a tough time justifying them to a prospect. You must sell yourself on the validity of the home's prices before you sell someone else, especially if that person is only shopping price. Any order-taker can give away the product or service at a lower price. The mark of a Superachiever is that he or she can represent the value of the homes and how they benefit the buyer, regardless of price.

Unless You Are Selling Commodities, Price Is Never the Only Concern

Suppose a farm produced 60,000 tons of soybeans and wholesaled the beans to three separate brokers for the same price. The three brokers then market the same beans from the same farm to a grocery store chain. Would the grocery store consider price as the only factor?

Say two of the three distributors offered the same product under the same terms but at a lower price than the third distributor. The third distributor, however, offers the following:

Service calls on a monthly basis—The other distributors don't make calls.

Delivery—The other distributors require the customer to pick up the soybeans.

A warranty—No warranty is offered by the other two. Every sale is final.

Terms—Buy from the other two distributors and it's a cash-only sale.

Remember, the beans come from the same farm, have the same grain, texture, and flavor. Yet, through differentiation in the form of value-added service, the third distributor is able to outsell the competition regardless of price.

The point of this example is to stress that if you differentiate yourself and your new homes, price will stop being the main concern of your prospects.

Why Buy?

There are several factors that influence a new home buyer.

The Sales Representative. Prospects usually meet you, the salesperson, before seeing the home. Within five seconds of seeing you, they have already formed a first impression. If, for whatever reason, they don't "buy" you, they probably won't buy what you're selling either. To customers, you represent and reflect the product, and the company, so you have tremendous influence over their decision to own.

Service. There are two types of sales organizations: those that are price driven and those that are service and value driven. The price-driven company and its salesperson operate on the "one-night-stand philosophy"—get in, sell, get out. This type of company does not care about developing customer relationships. Their primary market is a customer who shops for the lowest price, not service, and credibility.

On the other hand, the service-and-value-driven company places a high priority on establishing long-term customers and on soliciting referrals.

Not long ago, a company's representatives purchased two struggling new communities within 100 miles of my home. In talking with them, I learned that they travel the East Coast seeking distressed properties. When they hear of a developer in financial trouble, they check out the land and, if they feel it's marketable, they'll purchase it at a fraction of its cost. They have a standard marketing plan that advertises the property as a bargain. The owner sells it as is, offering no neighborhood amenities, no additional services, and no guarantees. When the community is sold out, the company is gone.

There isn't anything wrong with this, of course, and it does meet a demand in the marketplace. The point is that, as a salesperson of new homes, you must decide on the type of company you prefer to represent because that's the company you'll sell to your customers.

Delivery. If you can deliver your new homes within a timeframe that suits each prospect, that may be enough to offset their objections about price. For example, a customer who has sold his house and must move out by September 1 will place a lower priority on price if you guarantee that his new home will be ready for occupancy in August.

Warranties. Providing outstanding service and new home warranties help to overcome price sensitivity. This is also one way to differentiate your new homes and community from others your prospects may be considering.

When To Talk Money

For the most part, even if your prices are boldly displayed in your sales brochures, you must not discuss price until the end of your presentation. I am not suggesting evasiveness, but most prospects will think that the new home or homesite will always "cost too much" until you build value. This can only be accomplished by discussing the benefits throughout your presentation.

Here's an example of how to overcome the "How much is it?" question before you have a chance to fully explain what the prospect will get for his money.

With my former construction and housing development career, we were hands down the highest-priced builder for a variety of reasons. When you build homes that cost half a million to one million dollars, the materials used are of substantially better quality than those used in lesser-priced homes.

The predictable price question we heard early in the presentation was, "What does it cost per square foot to build?" (or) "What's your price per square foot?"

Even if your prices are boldly displayed in your sales brochures, you must not discuss price until the end of your presentation.

The way to handle price resistance is to kick the chair out from underneath the objection by answering the question before it's asked. In our business, we handled it like this:

Superachiever: "Mr. and Mrs. Prospect, before we begin, I'd like to mention most of our customers ask one question first and that is, "How much per square foot will it cost to construct our new home? Is that a question you have today?"
Prospect: "Yes, we are wondering about the cost per square foot."
Superachiever: "Fine. Then let's talk about it briefly. Unfortunately, the cost of your new home will not be determined by the square foot. What will determine the value of your home are the component parts, such as the materials used to construct it. There are major price differences in items such as floor coverings, fixtures, and exterior and interior finishes. What we need to first determine is what you would like in your home. Then we'll calculate the price, based upon the materials used. That makes sense, doesn't it?"

When to address the issue of price—not the actual price itself—is your call. If your homes are priced considerably higher than those of your competitors and you know the question will arise early, you may choose to address the objection early in your presentation.

Owners or Moaners

An intense desire to own reduces the price objection substantially. And yet, even those who strongly desire to own the lovely new home you're selling will still moan about it costing too much.

Unfortunately, a few people think that badgering salespeople is a sport and they're in to win. For others, negotiation is the name of the game. They feel the day's a total loss unless they can bargain your boots off.

With the something-for-nothing mentality prevalent today, many customers won't pay the price unless they feel that something extra has been thrown in for free. And, of course, there are those who habitually object to the price just to receive reassurance that they are getting the best value possible.

When you hear a prospect say, "It costs too much," try responding with "How much is too much?" or "How far apart are we?" These questions will give you some idea of what they think your new homes are worth and what they would prefer to pay.

When you know how your price compares to their preference, you'll be in a better position to respond to their objections.

Another way to answer an objection about the new home costing too much is to ask, "In comparison to what?" That might open the door for you to present the benefits of your community compared to another.

A successful salesperson I know adds another twist to the cost objection. She told me that, when her prospect says the price is too high, what she hears him say is that his desire is too low.

"So, I concentrate on increasing his desire to own rather than to argue with him about price," she said.

Reduction to the Ridiculous Close (Cost-Per-Day Close)

There is a world of difference between willingness to pay and ability to pay. Using the *Reduction to the Ridiculous Close* bridges the gap between the two.

Suppose a prospect likes one of your homes and one in another community. He tells you that he likes your home better but the other one is $10,000 less.

With the *Reduction to the Ridiculous Close*, you spread the difference over a period of time.

Prospect: "I really like your home, but $10,000 is a lot of money."
Superachiever, with calculator in hand: "I know $10,000 seems like a lot but let's break it down. You say the other house is $10,000 less. If you divided $10,000 by 30 years, the length of your mortgage, that's $333 a year. Divide that by 12 months and you get $27.75. Now, if you divide $27.75 by 30 days, you end up with 93 cents a day. Now,

let me ask you this. Are you spending that much on soda?
"Mr. Prospect, I know this might seem ridiculous, but if you think about it, that $10,000 really isn't that much when you consider you could own the home you really want and deserve for only 93 cents more a day. You're not going to let that stand in the way, are you?"

Money Close

Because financial terms are offered in the purchase of new homes and homesites, you can usually discover what part of the investment is causing the prospect to object if you break the terms into component parts.

1. **Total Investment** $_____
2. **Initial Investment** $_____
3. **Monthly Investment** $_____

> **Superachiever:** "Mr. Prospect, I sense your hesitancy, do you mind my asking is it the money?"
> **Prospect:** "Well, actually it is a little more than we anticipated."
> Break the money into component parts, to determine if it is the total investment, monthly investment or initial investment that is blocking the sale.
> **Superachiever:** "I can certainly understand, so why don't we take a look at the total offering?"

1. **Total Investment:** $_____   "Do you feel comfortable with the value?"
2. **Initial Investment:** $_____   "Is that amount comfortable or do you have that readily available?"
3. **Monthly Investment:** $_____   "How does that work with your budget?"

Additional Responses Regarding Price

1. **Your price is too high.**
   "In comparison to what?"
   "How much did you think it would cost?"
   "How high is too high?"
2. **You've got to do better than that.**
   "What do you mean better?"
   "How far apart are we?"
   "Are you saying you are prepared to make an offer?"

3. It costs too much.

"Today most things do. How much do you feel it should cost?"

4. I can get it for less from your competitor.

"I can appreciate that, Mr. Prospect. But that being the case, why haven't you purchased from them yet?"

Note: That's a bold response, but he will tell you what's preventing him from going to the competition.

CHAPTER 10

What's Here Today May be Home Tomorrow

Emotion is created by motion. If you doubt that, go into a room and pull all the curtains over the windows. Place a chair in the center of the room and sit there in the semi-darkness. After a few minutes, check your emotional pulse. Are you feeling energetic or lethargic? Happy or melancholy?

Now, open the curtains, turn on the lights, play some music, and dance as though nobody's looking. Now, how do you feel?

Move Prospects Forward

Usually, we allow our emotions to rule our motions. We cancel an appointment because we don't feel like going. We slam our fists down because we feel angry. We cry because we feel betrayed. We'll eat chocolate because we feel a craving. We end a relationship because we don't feel in love anymore. We all excuse doing something we should do by saying, "I just don't feel like it."

In reality, we would accomplish much more if we allowed our bodies to lead our emotions. When the body directs the mind, it creates patterns of movement that result in feelings of confidence, personal power, well being, and pleasure.

For example, if you wait until you're feeling confident to close sales, you'll let many slip through your fingers. If, regardless of how you feel, you force your body through the motions of closing, then the actions will create the emotion. With every sale you close, you will feel more confident.

The same principle applies to your prospects. They come into your sales center, look at your homes but don't feel like making a decision right now. Instead, they feel like putting it off until another day when they might be in a more decisive mood.

The salesperson's greatest hindrances to closing the sale are the prospects' indecisiveness and procrastination. It is common for customers to want to procrastinate and delay making a decision. In fact, many will do it even when they know that the home is exactly what they want or need. Why? Because they can.

Personnel consultant and public speaker Robert Half defines postponement as the most sincere form of rejection. He adds that it's a "sure bet that anything delayed will get further delayed."

Hesitant buyers frequently say:

▌ Do you have any additional information?
▌ We're in the initial stage and just beginning to look.
▌ We need to see one more home. (or) What else is available?
▌ We need to think it over.
▌ We must check with our advisors first.

These phrases indicate uncertainty. They don't feel confident enough to make a decision yet and want to delay it.

So, what do you do? Create motion to get emotion. The emotion they need to feel is a sense of urgency. You kindle that by showing them how circumstances might change if they delay making a decision to buy. The homesite they want may be sold. Interest rates may not remain as low. The home they've selected may increase in price. Conditions of the sale might change and not be as favorable as they are now.

Create action by walking the prospect through the home again. Review its features, the advantage of buying in this community, and the benefits of home ownership. Help the prospect to see the urgency of buying now rather than waiting until she feels like it. By then, it may be too late and she will regret not making the decision to buy when she had the opportunity.

Create motion to get emotion.

Urgency is not high-pressure selling or manipulation. It is simply conveying the honest facts that the prospect needs to know in order to make an informed decision about buying a new home. Some of these facts may be associated with deadlines; therefore, there is urgency connected with them.

Most of us dislike procrastinating and we regret having missed opportunities. It is personally satisfying to make a decision and move on. By showing prospects a sense of urgency, you keep them focused on the facts. You have demonstrated exactly what they should do and why. They may still not feel like buying, but at least you went through all the motions. They will know that what's here today, may be home (or gone) tomorrow.

The Fear of Loss and Desire for Gain

Your prospect's two strongest buying emotions are the fear of loss and the desire for gain.

The fear of loss causes prospects to feel they will miss out or lose if they do not own in your community. Also, people covet what they cannot have. In fact, most people do not even realize how badly they want to own one of your homes until it is suggested that they cannot have it.

Desire for gain is a function of your presentation and how you help prospects perceive— through their senses and emotions the lifestyle they will enjoy through owning in your community. The prospect is not so much buying a home or home-site as he is acquiring the perceived feelings of satisfaction or dream fulfillment that can be realized with ownership.

> *Your prospect's two strongest buying emotions are the fear of loss and the desire for gain.*

Transfer the Sense of Urgency

Judy, a top producer in a retirement community, called to say her sales were slow. When questioned as to the cause, she said she felt certain it was because there was no urgency. I asked if she believed a sale was a transfer of the salesperson's enthusiasm to the emotions of the customers.

Judy immediately assured me that her enthusiasm was not the problem. She understood the positive role it played in the sale.

Our discussion continued and centered on the fact that customers sense our emotions. If we are happy and excited, we transfer the same emotions to the customer by the way we act. Likewise, if we are negative and fearful, we transfer those emotions.

As we talked, Judy realized that, although she was enthusiastic about her new homes, she was losing sales because she was not transferring that sense of urgency. Her customers were not being motivated either by a legitimate fear of loss or a personal desire for gain. Somewhere in her presentation, she was dropping the ball by not expressing or stressing the limited availability of the homes they wanted to buy.

Urgency is an emotion that must be forwarded by us and felt by the prospect. There are many ways to convey urgency in selling new homes, but perhaps the most powerful method is to quote actual sales figures. If your community is selling three homes or homesites per week, you might quote that rate of sales at the beginning of your presentation, saying something like this:

Superachiever: "Mr. and Mrs. Prospect, before discussing our homes and the lifestyle our neighborhood will afford your family, you will notice on our community map the homesites that are tagged/ flagged in red. This indicates those that have already been sold. As you can see, we are quite busy at (community). As a matter of fact, we have three homes/homesites that are purchased daily/weekly by families/people just like you."

Quote your rate of sales throughout your presentation. If your prospects mention that it will be 30 days or more before they can buy, say:

Superachiever: "Mr. and Mrs. Prospect, as I mentioned, we have three families becoming owners in our community weekly. This means at the end of the month, the availability of homes/homesites will diminish by 12. I'm happy to show you today's best values, but please bear in mind that whatever you see today will, in all probability, not be available tomorrow."

This incorporates the emotional pull from both the desire of gain and the fear of loss. Urgency statements such as these may be conveyed throughout your sales presentation.

Ways to Create Urgency

One of a Kind. The most common form of urgency is the one-of-a-kind statement. People will buy nearly anything that they perceive to be one of a kind. The beauty of real estate is that, because of the uniqueness of every home, condominium, townhome or patio home, each one truly is one of a kind.

In discussing the fact that the property is one of a kind, it is important that you take the initiative to control inventory. Even if you have 75 homesites, you cannot possibly show that many at one time. Decide ahead of time which ones you will be showing.

If you have a tough time selecting the sites to show the prospect, think how difficult it will be for your prospect to decide. To keep him from being overwhelmed, narrow the choices to two or three. Failure to

Synergy Increases Urgency

Several years ago, I attended a seminar conducted by the Pacific Coast Institute. Though the topic was not urgency, the principle of synergy that was addressed offered a practical and powerful method of conveying urgency.

Consider that a mule is capable of pulling a load of approximately eight thousand pounds. Therefore, it would seem reasonable to assume two mules could manage sixteen thousand pounds. In actuality, two mules that have been trained to pull together can far exceed sixteen thousand pounds and easily handle eighteen to twenty thousand pounds.

So, how does this relate to sales? The application is this: If the entire sales team works in unison to create a sense of urgency, the effect will be greater.

Keep in mind that with adult learning, it takes six repetitions to attain a retention level of 62 percent. That means a key point during your presentation must be repeated six times before your prospect mentally absorbs it.

When conveying urgency to your prospects, they must hear urgency-building facts repeatedly during your presentation. Some of this can be accomplished by other team members. If you have your prospect in tow, she may hear another team member say to you, "Before you take your guest to the models or out to the property, I'm happy to say we've had another family join our community. Home (or homesite) number 142 is now sold and you should remove this fine property from your list of available homes (or homesites)."

do this forces your prospect to think it over and then he may decide not to own at all.

Increase in Property Values. A pricing strategy should be designed to assist sales momentum. By scheduling price adjustments in advance, developers and builders can give their sales team a good presentation point that causes immediate urgency. Increases in prices are normally structured within predevelopment or preconstruction stages and give early investors an advantage.

Prescheduled price increases can only be achieved with the controlled release of inventory during phrases of development. This avoids over supply and allows the opportunity to increase prices as sales occur, which stimulates buyers to act today rather than experience higher prices tomorrow.

Also, it will increase the values of homes and homesites already purchased. This gives you happy homeowners, who see an early return on investment. But more importantly, by controlling inventory to enhance values, a clear message is sent to buyers that the longer they procrastinate, the more the home may cost later.

Possession Dates and Scheduling. Move-in and possession are almost always part of the consideration in a decision to own a new home. If construction time is 90 to 120 days and the closing of their resale home is within the same time frame, then urgency is a top priority.

With second homes and vacation homes, possession and delivery can be of paramount importance if the home is to be completed in season for personal use or if rental income is important, especially if it is factored into the loan to qualify the prospect.

Production Schedules. When features—such as carpeting, appliances, and wall coverings—need to be selected, this presents you with an opportunity to move prospects ahead in the decision-making process. At a critical point in the sales conversation, you might say something to the effect of:

> **Superachiever:** "Mr. and Mrs. Prospect, I can appreciate your needing a little more time to think it over, but we are at a critical point in construction. Wall covering, carpet selection, and tiles must be selected now. You still have the opportunity to have your brand new home customized exclusively for you rather than having to settle for our decorator's taste."

Selling From Strength. In using urgency, it is important to sell from a position of strength, to appear indifferent about whether the prospect buys or doesn't buy.

Selling from strength uses the element of reverse psychology that makes people want something they may not be able to get. In other words, you create a need (desire for gain) and then indicate it may be hard to fulfill (fear of loss).

The Take Away Close

This is the preferred closing strategy when conveying urgency. You must possess and convey an "I don't care" attitude to be able to sell from strength. The point is, you really do not care if the prospect becomes involved, because regardless of whether she chooses to own or not, someone else is waiting for the opportunity to buy a new home from you.

This close is rooted in the prospect's fear of loss. Although you have fostered a desire for gain by giving a brilliant presentation, the prospects may still be hesitant and indecisive. So, rather than to continue speaking in terms of what the prospects gain, you shift gears. Now you speak in terms of what the prospects will lose by not taking action.

> **Superachiever:** "Mr. and Mrs. Prospect, I can see you are absolutely enthralled with this gorgeous homesite. But since you are unable to make up your mind, I have a suggestion that will help you avoid disappointment. As you are aware, this is the only homesite at this price. In the event someone else decides to purchase your homesite before you do, why don't we select another one almost as nice?"

Now remain perfectly silent so they can think about this. People do not know how badly they want something until you suggest they cannot have it.

> **Prospect:** "We don't want a homesite almost as nice."
> **Superachiever:** "I understand. The initial investment is only $_____. Will you be using cash or personal check today?"

Move into your closing sequence and conclude the transaction with the *Order Form Close.*

> NOTE: *This strategy may not work 100 percent of the time. Your prospect may respond with:*

> **Prospect:** "We'll take our chances" (or) "If it's meant to be, it's meant to be."
> **Superachiever:** "What! Are you sure that if someone were to take your homesite, that would be okay with you. You are willing to settle for second best? Mr. and Mrs. Prospect, you just don't seem like the type of people who would settle for second best. Are you?"

Prospect may respond with: "This is really pushing us." (or) "We are just not comfortable."

> **Superachiever:** "I understand. It's just that, in the past, so many people just like you have come back after a few days only to discover their homesites are now owned by someone else. I just don't want that to happen to you."

Your demeanor and presentation should suggest that you work in a community where customers eagerly await the opportunity to own a new home.

More Ways to Make It Happen

Closes

Here are additional powerhouse closing strategies to master.

1. My Lawyer or Accountant Close

The prospect tells you that your new home and the terms are perfect but, before he makes a final decision, he must run it by his lawyer or accountant.

When a prospect says he needs a third-party approval, either he is using a smoke-screen objection or he is controlled by his fears.

If he says he needs to solicit advice from a third party—such as a lawyer, accountant or financial advisor—he is really saying that he needs someone to assure him that it's a wise decision.

The *My Lawyer or Accountant Close* incorporates the closing strategy of subject to or conditional-terms selling.

> **Prospect:** "This seems to be the perfect solution *but*, before making my final decision, I need to run this by my accountant."
> **Superachiever:** "I can understand. Then am I correct in assuming you are totally satisfied, and there is no question in your mind that you feel it's the right thing for you to do?"
> **Prospect:** "Yes, I'm satisfied. I just want her to look it over."
> **Superachiever:** "Great, then the only question is whether your accountant says it's the right thing to do, is that correct?"

Prospect: "That's it."
Superachiever: "Mr. Prospect, may I ask you a question? (pause). Just suppose your accountant were present at this very moment and she advised you to take advantage of the offering. Would you act today?"
Prospect: "I suppose I would."
Superachiever: "Unfortunately, she is not with us today, but prior to your speaking with her and to facilitate the transaction in a timely fashion, let's prepare the paperwork now and we will make the sale subject to her final approval. This way, the process has begun and if, by chance, she doesn't agree, we will simply start over. That makes perfect sense, doesn't it?"

If the prospect agrees to the paperwork subject to, you can facilitate the details of the sale with the lawyer, accountant or advisor, answering questions, and overcoming the third party's objections personally.

2. Erroneous Conclusion Close

With this close you intentionally make an erroneous statement about a detail that has been decided upon and confirmed earlier in the sales conversation. When you purposely make the erroneous statement, the prospect will correct you and walk right into the sale.

Here's an example using the delivery date.

Superachiever: "Mr. Prospect, let me make sure I have all details. You require delivery on the 30th of the month. Is that correct?"
Prospect: "No, it must be delivered by the 15th."
Superachiever: "You're right. I apologize. I see it in my notes."

By correcting you, the prospect has closed the sale with his own words and you now conclude the transaction.

3. Maybe I Should Wait Close

This close is sometimes referred to as the *Timing is Not Right Close*. This is a method for overcoming procrastination or uncovering a smoke-screen objection. There are two ways to address the *Maybe I Should Wait* statement. The first is to answer it with a question:

Prospect: "I'm not sure of the timing. Maybe I should wait six months."
Superachiever: "Maybe you should, Mr. Prospect. May I ask a question though?"
Prospect: "Sure."
Superachiever: "What will be different six months from now?" (Remain silent and listen for the concerns and final objections. It may

just be a matter of offering concessions such as terms. Listen carefully and the prospect may reveal something minor that you can overcome.)

You may also answer "Maybe I Should Wait" with Zig Ziglar's famous close:

Prospect: "Maybe I should wait."
Superachiever: Maybe you *should* wait. Because anytime you make a decision to invest in something there is always a possibility of loss.

"I know there are a couple of things in my life that probably would have been better off had I waited. I know when my wife and I got married, had we waited, we could have had a honeymoon to end all honeymoons.

"I know when we had our first child it wasn't the right timing. Had we waited a few years we could have given him anything he wanted.

"And I know if I had waited when I purchased my first home, I could have built a really nice first home. Before you venture out of town, the problem with waiting until all the lights are green is, you just might spend your entire life where you are. If you wait until everything is just right, you will never own anything you are entitled to own and enjoy.

"Since you want it, and it will be of benefit to you, can you really think of any reason why you shouldn't treat yourself and your family to what you all deserve? The initial investment is only 10 percent. Will you be using a credit card or check today?"

4. Ultimatum Close/Final Decision Close

This is the close where you issue your final proposal. This technique requires confidence and strength with the attitude that no one sale will break your career or make your day.

You've made multiple calls and presentations to a prospect who keeps saying, "We'll get back to you." In addition, she keeps requesting information and "time to think about it."

You have invested considerable time, much more than normal. The prospect has all the information, yet she can't seem to make a decision. It's time to issue the ultimatum—the *Final Decision Close.*

You prepare the contracts in their entirety with the same information you have discussed and you take them to the prospect and say:

Superachiever: "Ms. Prospect, we have covered every issue and concern. You have an immense amount of time invested and so do I. Either this is a good idea or it is not. One way or another, let's reach a positive outcome right now."

Take your contract and pen and hand it to the prospect.

> **Superachiever:** "If you authorize the contract, I'll get your new home ready for delivery by the first of the month." (Remain perfectly silent.)
>
> Regardless of the outcome, at least you are through chasing phantoms and wasting time.

I shared this close with a Fortune 500 Company and they customized the technique to use for their mailing list. It seems they had two lists, one for those who regularly purchased and another for those who never purchased. Yet, they continued to mail the same brochures and information to the people on both lists.

They applied the *Ultimatum Close* and designed a letter with a postage-paid response card. The letter in essence said: "Through the years we have mailed you information without your response. If you wish to continue receiving brochures and information, please return the postcard and we will keep you on the list. Otherwise, this is our last contact."

The response was overwhelming. Most did not reply, but they saved a fortune in brochures and postage and redirected their savings to new prospects and customers who purchased. They now send this ultimatum mailing annually.

5. Mercedes Close

People usually want what they can't have or afford. Sometimes, if a person is financially unable to own the waterfront home, he would rather not own a home at all.

It's called champagne-and-caviar taste on a beer-and-pretzel budget.

For the prospect who insists on only owning the best regardless of his qualifications, try this:

> **Superachiever:** "Mr. Prospect, recently I invested in a new automobile. It was a brand new Nissan Maxima. Ideally though, I wanted to own a Mercedes Benz. Like you, I only want to own the best, yet financially I wasn't ready. It's not that the Mercedes was unaffordable, it just wasn't prudent."
>
> "One day I will drive the Mercedes, but right now I'm driving what makes perfect sense and it takes me where I want to go in fine style."
>
> "I understand what you're saying about wanting to own the waterfront home. It's absolutely lovely but, rather than deny yourself ownership and its benefits entirely, why don't you start with what's prudent.

Buy the home on the cul-de-sac. Later, when it makes more sense financially, you can sell that home and use the equity to purchase another home, maybe one on the water. Mr. Prospect, shall I complete the contract now?"

6. I'm Still Shopping Close

The *I'm Still Shopping Close* is used when a prospect says he wants to compare your price and offer with the competition before making a decision. In some cases, this is an unavoidable objection because there are those who simply enjoy the process of shopping and negotiating.

The key to this close is that you must give a sound reason why he should not go through the agony and spend the time going from neighborhood to neighborhood trying to find a better price.

The following technique is especially effective if the company you represent has been in business for several years and dominates the market.

> **Prospect:** "Before I make the final decision, I would like to shop around to be sure I'm getting the best possible price."
> **Superachiever:** "Mr. Prospect, I can certainly appreciate your wanting to shop for the best possible value. That's just smart business. I would like to make you aware, however, that we have been in business for 12 years and have helped many people just like you. As a matter of fact, most of our business is from repeat customers and referrals who had shopped around extensively for brand new homes before making their final decision and buying with us. Why put yourself through the agony of trying to locate a better value, when smart shoppers just like you have already performed the shopping for you? Let's go ahead and wrap up the details now."

Another method to combat "I'm shopping around" is to offer an incentive or a "today only special." A small builder where I live gives potential home buyers a 15-day price guarantee when they want to shop around. After that, the price increases by several thousand dollars. He says that, by putting a time frame on it, they must compress their comparison shopping time into two weeks. Frequently, however, they decide to avoid the hassle and they buy on the spot.

As a value-added selling tool, another builder provides buyers with an extended home shield warranty that offers added protection for systems and appliances. This is the same builder who, in his advertising, invites customers to compare and come back.

A third strategy to combat shopping around is *The Always Be Last Close*. When you are absolutely convinced your prospect will be shopping, always be the last community on the list.

With this close never argue, but congenially issue the invitation to shop.

> **Superachiever:** "Mr. Prospect, I understand you need to check other availabilities and prices. However, before you go shopping, I was wondering if you are not the type of person who makes instantaneous buying decisions."
> **Prospect:** "No. That's why I want to shop."
> **Superachiever:** "Great, then will you promise me something? Before you make your final choice, come back to see me and I promise you will receive the best value possible."
> **Prospect:** "Sure, I'll not make the final decision without checking with you first."

The idea that you may be able to offer a better value will entice the prospect back to you before rendering a final decision.

In some cases, the prospect will say, "Why don't you just give me your best price now?"

Resist the temptation to give in or you may never see the prospect again, because it's possible he will use your final price to negotiate with the competition. Instead say:

> **Superachiever:** "Go out and get the best price you can and then come back and see me. I'm certain, when all is said and done, I'll be the one to give you the very best value."

When the prospect does come back to see if you can beat the best price he received, by all means be ready to do it, if possible. If you cannot beat the price, explain it's because you have the better value in a new home, which includes warranty, delivery, additional features, and a host of other value-added services.

> **Superachiever:** "You're right. It is a higher price, but look at what you receive. It includes the extended warranty; granite countertops; tiled foyer; kitchen, and baths; as well as custom-built, solid wood cabinetry. Mr. Prospect, you do want to begin enjoying the benefits today, don't you?"

This is also an example of the *Cork Close*, a final strategy to use when prospects are shopping and comparing new homes. It illustrates that there are two values to every investment. One is its actual cost and the other is what its value is to the buyer.

Greater Value

When Shirley and her husband moved to Maryland several years ago, they were boating in a wooden Chris Craft around the Inner Harbor when they hit something submerged in the water and the boat began sinking. They radioed for help.

The Coast Guard arrived, located the hole in the boat, and plugged it with cork, which kept the boat from sinking. At that moment, the value of the cork was not 30 cents a pound.

7. The Summary Close

As you approach the end of your presentation, the prospect is faced with the task of having to arrange all of your information into a clear and concise picture before she is able to make a decision about owning.

As I stated before, you are always selling benefits, so you must summarize them in a manner that proves your new home meets her needs.

Here is the four-step process to develop your *Summary Close*:

**Step 1 Bridge into Your Summary Close
with a Transition Statement**

Superachiever: "Ms. Prospect, we have covered a lot of territory today! Before moving forward, let's review the highlights of our discussion."

**Step 2 Reconfirm Your Prospect's Wants, Needs,
and Desires**

Superachiever: "You mentioned you loved the area and the neighborhood is convenient to the school district. Is that correct?"
Superachiever: "Your primary concern is that your move must coincide with the start of school. Is that on target?"
Superachiever: "And, of course, because of the sale of your existing home, you would prefer that I assist you with the details of locating an aggressive brokerage company. Have I included everything?"

**Step 3 Summarize How Your Product or Service
Meets the Prospect's Wants, Needs, and Desires**

Superachiever: "To assure on-time delivery, we will begin by scheduling a meeting with our design consultant. Once there, you will make your selections and, when finalized, you will have your brand new home customized to reflect your unique living requirements."

"Concerning customization, based on past experience, if you choose the energy efficient program, you can expect 15 percent savings on your heating and cooling bills. In many cases, the savings are even greater."

"Now, the best part of this proposal is the terms. With a small initial investment of $_____ the balance of your 10 percent deposit will be due when the builder starts your new home."

Step 4 Ask for the Order and Close the Sale
(*Tie Down Close*)

Superachiever: "I have taken the liberty to prepare the paperwork. All that's necessary is your authorization."

A common question aspiring Superachievers ask is how to actually transition to the final closing sequence. The *Summary Close* is the perfect method to bridge into your final close. You summarize the benefits, even if there are as many as 20 or more items, and say, "When would you like to get started?" (or) "Why don't you give it a try." (or) "The initial investment is 10 percent. Will that be cash or check?" If acceptance is gained, you simply conclude the sale with *The Order Form Close*. If an objection is offered, you identify and overcome the final objection, then close the sale.

8. Paint A Fantasy Picture Close

We are all sensitive and receptive to the suggestive influences of the people around us. In sales, this has particular significance because it means when you are excited, your excitement and enthusiasm are contagious and will be transferred to the buyer.

> *Your excitement and enthusiasm are contagious and will be transferred to the buyer.*

The *Paint A Fantasy Picture Close* piggybacks on the *Assumptive Close* in that you speak to the prospects as though they already own the new home. Your enthusiastic suggestions will actually paint vivid mental pictures of what it is going to be like to live in the neighborhood and own a new home.

With the *Paint A Fantasy Close*, you enthusiastically create mental images in the minds of your prospects of what it's going to be like to use, benefit and enjoy the new home and community. As a result, your suggestions move them immediately into the mindset of ownership.

Paint a Picture and They Will Buy

Luci and her husband, Ben, were shopping for a new home in a Maryland suburb. They had already gone to the bank to get prequalified so they knew how much they could afford. There was some urgency in buying a new home because Luci and Ben were expecting their first child in seven months.

At one of the communities they visited, a salesperson began showing them one of the model homes. Not long after the demonstration began, Luci commented on the fact that they were expecting a baby in November.

The salesperson immediately stopped the home demonstration.

"Wait!" she said. "We're looking at the wrong house."

She then walked them over to another model, one a little larger but still affordable.

"This model is perfect for you," the salesperson said. Then, she began to show them how the kitchen was large and how its layout would accommodate a highchair and playpen. She pointed to the dining room downstairs, commenting that it would make an ideal playroom and had pocket doors that could be closed when company came. And she noted that one of the bedrooms upstairs was directly across the hall from the master bedroom, Luci and Ben would be within earshot of their child.

She mentioned that the laundry room was upstairs, near the bedrooms, so they would be able to place the baby in the nearby crib while they washed and folded the clothes. And she showed them on the map where the community playground would be built.

The salesperson talked enthusiastically about baby's first Christmas in the house and where they could place the Christmas tree so the lights would be visible outside. She asked about the grandparents and if they would be staying with them during the holidays.

A mother of three herself, the salesperson knew exactly what features would interest a mom-to-be, so she was able to paint a fantasy picture of life with a little one in this new home. She wasn't just using it as a ploy to get them to buy, though. She really believed that this was the perfect home for Luci and Ben.

When the presentation was over, the salesperson explained that they needed to decide soon if they wanted the house because it would take six months to build it and their baby was due in seven. Luci and Ben were sold and signed that day.

Examples of Paint a Fantasy

Superachiever: "Mr. and Mrs. Prospect, your children and grandchildren will love spending summer days with you around the community pool, won't they?"

Superachiever: "Close your eyes. Picture yourself relaxing on your patio (or outdoor living area), enjoying the sun during the day and then capping the evening off with a view of a romantic sunset. That's the homesite you really want, isn't it?"

Superachiever: "Can't you just smell the steaks on the grill as you enjoy weekends at your very own mountain retreat?"

9. Lost Sale Close

This one is sometimes referred to as the *Doorknob Close.*

You have delivered your presentation, used your best closing strategies, and yet it seems hopeless that the prospect will make a decision. Begin this close by packing up your paperwork and thanking him for his time. Act like you realize the situation is hopeless and you are giving up. When the prospect thinks you are going to leave and the presentation is over, his buying resistance drops.

While you are seated with your packed briefcase or standing ready to reach for the doorknob, say:

Superachiever: "Mr. Prospect, I realize you are not going to own a brand new home today, but I wonder if you could help me with my presentation. Could you share with me the reason you are not going to buy today? I don't want to make the same mistake again that I have made with you. What's the real reason for not owning today?"

Remain perfectly silent and listen carefully for his real reason as well as for hot buttons you may have missed. The prospect, now relieved of tension, will usually tell you the hidden concerns or reasons why he is not going to purchase. After obtaining the real reason (final objection) sit back down and say:

Superachiever: "Mr. Prospect, thank you. I'm so glad you brought that to my attention. Obviously, I did not explain that portion of the presentation very well. May I make an attempt to explain that one more time?" (Start your presentation over.)

Most salespeople, out of fear, will not go the extra mile with this final closing attempt. But it has worked for me. I have retrieved at least a dozen seemingly lost sales from qualified customers who would not reveal their hidden reason for moving forward until I used this final closing method.

The Sales Process Begins
When You Hear Your First Objection

Your ability to handle objections with ease will determine how many sales you actually close. These closing strategies, along with those mentioned in previous chapters, will give you a heads up with your prospects and get you to Yes quicker.

A friend of mine recently returned from a trip to New York, where she encountered all types of street salespeople. What intrigued her was that their sales pitch and their products matched their locations.

Those near the theater district were louder and walking up to people in the street to sell everything from bootlegged show tickets to T-shirts. A vendor near the major department stores had positioned himself at an intersection and was selling pocketbooks for $5 each from a crate-sized box filled to overflowing.

> *Your ability to handle objections with ease will determine how many sales you actually close.*

Near Soho—an area of boutiques, antique shops, and specialty restaurants—a man was quietly selling "fine" jewelry showcased on black velvet.

I relate this story to stress the importance in sales of matching your product, presentation, and personality.

Whenever you deliver a presentation to a prospect, you become part of that person's buying experience. Therefore, you want it to be an honest representation of yourself.

The closing strategies in this book are intended to be conformed to you. As you internalize them, they become part of who you are and help you become who you want to be. Use them well and wisely, because they will work if you do.

The choice is yours. You can make good or make excuses.

CHAPTER 12

What To Say When You Aren't Sure What To Say

There are times when you'll be ready to close the sale and, instead of objections, the prospect will ask you questions or try to negotiate. In anticipation of this, I've listed some common situations and effective ways you can respond.

Prospect: "Will you discount (cut) your commission?"
Superachiever: "I can appreciate why you're asking and I'll be up front with you and say no. I will not adjust my fees for this reason. As a professional, my time has a certain value and I only work with people like you, who realize the value of professional service."
(or)
Superachiever: "Please do not think of what I earn as a commission. My earnings are based on a fee for service and I can promise you my service far outweighs the fee."

Prospect: "Will you adjust your commission? Your competition will."
Superachiever: "You're right, Mr. Prospect. There are a lot of desperate sales representatives out there and I'm concerned. May I share why? A person who doesn't see the value in himself and in his service will not value you either."
Prospect: "Will you take less than the listed price? (or) What's the best you can do? (or) What's the bottom line?"
Superachiever: "Are you saying you like this home/homesite and would like to own it?"
Prospect: "Yes, but only if we can get it at the right price. (or) Yes, if we can get a deal."
Superachiever: "Mr. Prospect, let me ask you this. When you move into your new home and meet your neighbor who says, "How much of a discount did you get?" or "What kind of a deal did they give you?", how are you going to feel? The reality is if we offered discounts to everyone, your neighbor might look at you and say, "Is

that all?" At this point, how would you really feel? I sense now that you understand why we don't negotiate. Everyone who owns in (community) gets the same great value. After all, that's what's really important, isn't it?"

Prospect: "I'm only concerned about the deal I get. If my neighbors get a better price, then good for them. (or) I've never paid full price for real estate before."

Superachiever: "I'm curious. Are you familiar with how real estate's true value is determined? In reality, the developer/builder or the salesperson representing the home/homesite does not determine value. Value is based on comparable sales. In other words, a professional appraiser says property is only worth the last price for which a home was purchased. If yesterday, someone purchased a comparable home/homesite at $_____ and today you purchase it at $_____, then what is its true value? Mr. Prospect, we offer value protection and feel everyone should pay the same fair price. Wouldn't you agree?"

Prospect: "I did not bring my checkbook."

Superachiever: "That's fine. You say you would like to own and are prepared to proceed forward, except you do not have your checkbook?"

NOTE: It is important you ask the question, to confirm if the checkbook is the only reason prohibiting ownership.

Prospect: "Yes. That's right."

Superachiever: "I understand. So, we can still go ahead and start the paperwork. Any denomination of cash will serve as a good-faith deposit and place a hold on this particular home/homesite. What amount do you have available today?"

Prospect: "I did not bring my checkbook and I don't have cash."

Superachiever: "That's fine. Are you saying you would like to own and are prepared to proceed forward, except that you do not have your checkbook or any cash available?"

Prospect: "Yes."

Superachiever: "No problem. We won't let this prohibit ownership of your brand new home. Let's go ahead and prepare the paperwork and then I'll place your home on hold for 24 hours. Tomorrow morning I'll drop by to pick up a check or you can bring one to our office. What would be more convenient for you? Should I drop by or will you bring the deposit check to me?"

Prospect: "I have a good friend in the business."

Superachiever: "I can appreciate that, so I can understand your frustration of feeling obligated to do business with your friend. Yet, from a friendship perspective, you owe your friend your friendship.

From a business perspective, you owe yourself the best representative available. You do want the best working for you, don't you?"
Prospect: "Yes."
Superachiever: "Your friend will want the very best for you too, won't he?"

Prospect: "Why should I choose you or your company?"
The only way to answer this objection is for you to take the time to identify your strengths and differentiate yourself from the competition. I leave this one up to you. However, most consumers see a salesperson as a commodity. They feel we're all alike—one is the same as the other. If you have not justified to yourself why a prospect would choose you, then certainly the prospect won't be able to understand why he should choose you either.

When you're talking about your company, mention its reputation, years in business, community-minded, and philanthropic endeavors, areas of specialty, stability of its owners, etc. If you feel you have an advantage in the marketplace, state it clearly. However, don't get so caught up in communicating your company's attributes that you neglect to focus on how they benefit the prospect.

A friend who has worked in advertising for decades calls consumers "bellybutton gazers." "Their focus is always on themselves," she says. "They want to know how they can benefit from what you're selling."

The simple way to differentiate your company from its competitors is by showing prospects how they benefit by choosing you and the neighborhood you represent.

Prospect: "I'll buy an older house."
Superachiever: "Are you willing to take that kind of risk?"
(or)
Superachiever: "Are you willing to sacrifice the peace of mind that accompanies factory warranties and guarantees? And, just as important, why would you want to settle for someone else's taste in floor plans and decorating? With a brand new home, you can customize and personalize it to your specific living requirements and decorate it to reflect your unique taste."

Prospect: "Do you have a brochure and/or price list?"
Superachiever: "Certainly. I would like to customize a brochure package just for you. Please come in, tell me exactly what you are looking for and I'll put together your information and have you back on the road in two to three minutes."

Buy By Looking

People shop by brochures, but buy by looking. Research has shown that 75 percent of all brochures end up in a trash can within 72 hours.

Prospect: "I'm just looking."
Superachiever: "Wonderful! It's really a lot of fun looking at new homes and new communities, isn't it?"

NOTE: If the prospect responds with a No, then you have received your ultimate opportunity because that means she is tired and frustrated with shopping and nearing the end of her buying process.

Prospect: "Yes."
Superachiever: "Have you looked at any communities you especially like? (or) Tell me what kind/type of new home/community you are looking for?"

_____

Prospect: "We only have a few minutes."
Superachiever: "I understand. Many of our best customers who became happy homeowners said exactly the same thing. If you have just two or three minutes, let me give you a quick overview to save you valuable time."

(or)

Superachiever: "I understand and, since you only have a few minutes, I'll make certain you receive some literature, visit our models, and get back on the road quickly. Let me take just a moment and give you a quick overview of the location of our community, its amenities and floor plans."

_____

Prospect: "We have just started shopping."
Superachiever: "Outstanding! Then you have come to the right neighborhood first. I can prepare you with good information, show you our amenities, and homes and then you can use (community) as the standard of measure while you evaluate the other communities you'll shop. That's just smart business, isn't it?"

_____

Prospect: "I'm in a hurry. My spouse is waiting in the car."
Superachiever: "Let's walk out to the car and give your husband/wife/family a quick 60-second overview and perhaps we can prompt them to come in."

_____

Prospect: "Do you have a price list?"

Superachiever: "Ms. Prospect, our homes/homesites range from $_____ to $_____. Is that the investment range you were considering?"

NOTE: *If they say it's not a comfortable range, then ask, "How much are you considering?"*

Superachiever: "Mr. and Mrs. Prospect, I'm excited to assemble a brochure for you. However, I will not be including a price list. May I explain why? As shown on our plat map, the red flags indicate sold properties. As a matter of fact, our rate of sale is ___ new homes/homesites per week. The reason we do not include a price list is because whatever is available today will, in all probability, be gone tomorrow. Also, as rapidly as properties are moving, we never know when to expect a price increase. What I'm going to include in your brochure are the price ranges you desire and I'll call you periodically with the status of sold properties and price increases."

NOTE: *The psychology of follow-up is that the prospect must have a reason to come back/call back and the salesperson must have a reason to call back/invite back. It is vital to understand the strategy of withholding information. If you give the critical information, such as a price sheet, the prospect no longer needs your assistance and has no reason to come back to your sales center/model home.*

Specific Situations & Greetings

Multiple Groups. When several prospective buyers converge at one time, you should greet them collectively and attempt to discover who is a genuine prospect.

Superachiever: "Hi. Welcome to _____. My name is _____. As you can see, we are always busy at _____. Why don't you gather around and I'll give you a brief group presentation and assemble literature for those who may be interested. Oh, by the way, who is interested in owning a new home or homesite?"

———————

Agency Disclosure. Agency disclosure is mandatory. Your entire strategy is to comply with the requirements without complicating the process.

Superachiever: "Hi. It's a great day, isn't it? Welcome to _____. My name is _____ and you are . . .? Before giving you a brief overview, I represent the (builder/developer). Are you familiar with the state of _____'s agency disclosure form?"

———————

The Separating Couple. Remember, in most cases, it takes both the husband and the wife, or the significant others to render a decision. Many times, at the beginning or during your presentation, a couple may separate. You must keep them together initially to give them both a quick overview and to at least start them in the right direction before they begin their process-of-elimination shopping.

> **Superachiever:** "Mary, John, if just for the first few minutes, you would both stick with me, I'm going to give you a quick overview of our community as well as the amenities and the floor plans our builders offer. After that, please make yourself at home and look in any direction you would like to go at your leisure. But for now, stick with me, please."

The Realtor does all the talking. Initiate a "be honest" approach. The cooperating broker has good reason to be defensive. It's his or her customer and he or she has every right to want to maintain control.

> **Superachiever:** "Welcome to _____. My name is ____ and yours is . . .?"

The Realtor will either verbally identify herself or hand you her card.

> **Superachiever:** "Thank you, Ms. Realtor. It's good to meet you. And your customer's name is...? Welcome, Mr. and Mrs. Customer. You are very lucky to be with Mrs. Realtor. By reputation, she is one of the finest professionals in the area and you are fortunate to have someone as knowledgeable to assist you."
>
> **Superachiever:** "I'm sure you both are in a hurry, so I'll make sure you receive a brochure and see our models at your leisure. However, I'd like to take just a moment and give you a brief overview about our location, amenities and homes/homesites."

Or you could compliment the Realtor in front of the prospect and say:

> **Superachiever:** "Mrs. Realtor is an expert on the general area of our town, while I'm the resident expert on the specifics of this community. I'm sure Mrs. Realtor and I together can provide you with all the important information you will need for an informed decision."

Learn a Lesson from Abraham Lincoln

As an attorney, his strategy for winning a debate was to determine the issues of the counter-party in advance. Then he would develop his questions and answers and present the case to himself from their point of view. Like Lincoln, don't go into a situation unprepared.

A Closing Thought

Every profession in the world has its own failure rate. However, sales is the only profession in the world in which the normal rate of failure can be as high as 80 to 90 percent. When the economy has flatlined and competition is vicious, the rate is even greater.

In a booming economy, the sales profession is alluring; but when the economic indicators take a nosedive, things get a little trickier. The bad news is that you must work harder to convert prospects into buyers. The good news is that you have more time to do it because there aren't as many people buying homes.

Even in a tough economy, you can be a Superachiever if you avoid self-sabotage and practice persistence. Use the down cycles as opportunities to fine-tune your skills and to lay the groundwork for future sales.

Don't Be an Elephant or a Flea

When a baby elephant is first placed in a circus, its trainer ties a small rope around its leg and tethers it to a pole to keep it from running away. If the elephant strains to get free, at that age the rope is strong enough to hold it. As the elephant matures, the size of the rope remains the same because, by then, it is already conditioned to believe that it cannot break away so it won't try.

If you put a handful of fleas in a jar and screw on the lid, they will keep jumping against the lid to try to get out. However, after a few minutes, they stop. If you remove the lid, the fleas remain in the jar. Like the elephants, they are conditioned to their confinement and no longer test their boundaries.

How about you? What is holding you back? Have previous failures doused your enthusiasm and capped your confidence? Do you have limiting beliefs? Are you conditioned to accept imaginary boundaries?

Wilma Rudolph wasn't. Born prematurely and weighing less than five pounds, she was the 20th of 22 children. Because of racial segregation, she and her mother weren't allowed in the all-white hospital so her mother nursed her at home through many ailments, including scarlet fever and polio. From age six, she did exercises to strengthen her deformed legs and by age 12, could finally walk normally, without the crutches, brace or corrective shoes. That was when she decided to become an athlete.

In high school she set state records as a basketball star. Then she became a track star, attending her first Olympic Games in 1956 at age 16 and winning a bronze medal in the 4x4 relay. She went to Rome in 1960 and became the first American woman to win three gold medals in the Olympics. She won the 100-meter dash, the 200-meter dash and ran the anchor on the 400-meter relay team.

It's Amazing What We Can Accomplish If We Don't Know What Can't be Done

Colonel Sanders of Kentucky Fried Chicken was retired and over 60-years-old before he decided to make his recipe known. He made nearly 1,000 calls and spent nights in his car before he made his first sale.

At age 22, Rudyard Kipling published more than 70 of his short stories in seven paperback volumes.

In the two hours it took his client to drive from Milwaukee to his studio, Frank Lloyd Wright designed the house called Fallingwater. One of his most widely acclaimed homes, it was built over a rushing stream and a waterfall.

After celebrating her 100th birthday, Grandma Moses completed 25 more paintings.

Susan Butcher won the 16-day Iditarod dog-sled race by three minutes and 43 seconds, covering more than 1,049 miles in 70 degree-below-zero temperatures and 100 mile-per-hour winds.

You don't know what you can do until you do it. Businessman C. E. Welch of Welch's Grape Juice explained it this way:

> "Many men fail because they quit too soon. They lose faith when the signs are against them. They do not have the courage to hold on, to keep fighting in spite of that which seems insurmountable. If more of us would strike out and attempt the 'impossible,' we very soon would find the truth of that old saw that nothing is impossible. Abolish fear and you can accomplish anything you wish."

Chart of Closes

Name of Close	When to Use It
Order Form Close	Use this close at the beginning and during your presentation, when the prospect asks a question that indicates a buying signal; record the answer on the contract order form.
I Want to Think About It Close	Use this close to tread past the "Valley of Vague Generality" into the "Land of the Final Objection."
Money Close	Use this close to determine if it is the total investment, monthly investment, or initial investment that is blocking the sale.
Invitational Close	Use this close to conclude the sale either at the end or during the presentation. Invite the customer to try it out.
Hot Button Close	Use this close throughout the presentation. Press the prospects' hot buttons over and over to find out what will make them want to purchase your new homes.
Assumptive Close	Use this close once the demonstration is complete. Immediately pull out the contract and start filling it out.
Assumptive Handshake Close	Use this close to conclude the sale. The idea is that a hand-shake represents a person's word and psychologically bonds an agreement. *Note: this is a variation of the Assumptive Close.*
Alternatives Close	Use this close to automatically conclude the sale.
Trial Close	Use this close during the presentation to determine where you are with your prospect.
Ben Franklin Close	Use this close throughout the presentation with indecisive prospects to help them overcome certain concerns. This close should not be limited to the end of your presentation.

Name of Close	When to Use It
Puppy Dog Close	Use this close throughout the presentation. Take the potential buyer out to the property, allow them to walk around, see the décor, inhale the new house smell, touch the wallpaper, and get emotionally involved.
Sharp Angle Close	Use this close to handle smoke-screen objections. It helps unearth hidden objection.
Pancake Close	Use one close, and then jump to others in rapid succession before concluding the sale.
Minor Point Close	Use this close to allow customers to become accustomed to making smaller decisions before they are asked to make a major commitment to buy a new home or homesite. *Note: this close is often referred to as the Secondary Close.*
Yes Momentum Close	Use this close throughout the presentation. Ask customers questions that lead to a yes answer. Allow them to get in the mental pattern of saying yes at the beginning of the presentation, by the end of the closing, it will be difficult to say no.
Referral Prospecting Close	Use this close immediately after the purchase of the new home/homesite or at the time of delivery.
Reduction to the Ridiculous (Cost-Per-Day Close)	Use this close to bridge the gap between a customer's willingness to pay and ability to pay.
Take Away Close	Use this close to convey urgency. Your demeanor and presentation should suggest that you work in a community where customers eagerly await the opportunity to own a new home.
Lawyer or Accountant Close	Use this close when the prospect needs third party approval, to assure him that it's a wise decision.

Name of Close	When to Use It
Erroneous Conclusion Close	Use this close to make the prospect walk right into the sale. Purposely make an erroneous statement about a detail that has been decided and confirmed in earlier conversation, the prospect will correct you and walk right into the close.
Maybe I Should Wait Close	Use this close to overcome procrastination or uncovering a smoke-screen objection.
Ultimatum Close	Use this close to issue your final proposal when you have invested considerable time, much more than normal and the prospect can't seem to make a decision.
Mercedes Close	Use this close for the prospect that insists on owning the best regardless of his qualifications.
I'm Still Shopping Close	Use this close when the prospect wants to compare prices with the competition before making a decision.
The Always Be Last Close	Use this close when you are absolutely convinced your prospect will be shopping; always be the last community on the list.
The Summary Close	Use this close as you approach the end of your presentation. Arrange all your information into a clear and concise picture.
Paint a Fantasy Picture Close	Use this close to enthusiastically create mental images in the minds of your prospects. Make him visualize what it's going to be like to use, benefit and enjoy the new home and community.
Lost Sale Close	Use this close when nothing else seems to work. Begin this close by packing up your paperwork and thanking the prospect for their time. As you start to leave, the prospect will let down their resistance, giving you another opportunity to close the sale.

Resources

Recommended Reading

Manager's Books

Alfriend, Bonnie and Richard Tiller. *New Homes Sales Management.* Alfriend and Associates, Inc., 1996.

Blanchard, Ken and Sheldon Bowles. *Raving Fans.* William Morrow & Co, May 1993.

Blanchard, Ken and Sheldon Bowles. *Who Moved My Cheese?* Putnam Pub Group, September 1998.

Greenberg, Alan C. *Memos From the Chairman.* Workman Publishing Company, 1996.

Goldratt, Eliyahu M. *The Goal,* 2nd Edition. HighBridge Company, 2000.

Radice, Dennis. *The Homebuilders Sales Management Tool Kit.* BuilderBooks, 1999.

Sales Books

Alfriend, Bonnie. *Secrets of the Superstars.* Alfriend and Associates, Inc., 1993.

Barnes, Myers. *Reach The Top In New Home & Neighborhood Sales.* MBA Publications, 1999.

Barnes, Myers. *From Good To Great In New Home & Neighborhood Sales.* MBA Publishing, 2002.

Barnes, Myers. *Closing Strong, The Super Sales Handbook.* MBA Publishing, 1997.

Betcher, Frank. *How I Raised Myself From Failure to Success.* Simon & Schuster, 1992.

Kilpatrick, John A. *Understanding House Construction,* 2nd Edition. BuilderBooks, 1993.

Maxwell, John. *Failing Forward.* Thomas Nelson, 2000.

Pinto, Rick. *Success Is A Choice.* Bantam Doubleday Dell Pub, 1998.

Qubein, Nido. *Stairway to Success.* Executive Books, John Wiley & Sons, 1997.

Schultz, Bob. *The Official Handbook For New Home Sales People.* New Home Specialist, 1997.

Schultz , Bob. *Smart Selling Techniques.* New Home Specialist Publishing Group, 1998.

Tracy , Brian. *Advanced Selling Strategies.* Fireside, 1996.

Tracy, Brian. *Maximum Achievement.* Fireside, 1995.

Audio Programs

Dawson, Roger. *Secrets of Power Negotiation.* Nightingale-Conant Corporation, 1989.

Tracy, Brian. *The Psychology of Selling.* Nightingale-Conant Corporation, 2002.

Tracy, Brian. *The Universal Laws of Success.* Nightingale-Conant Corporation.

Tracy, Brian. *The Psychology of Achievement.* Nightingale-Conant Corporation, 2002.

Waitley, Dennis. *The Psychology of Winning.* Nightingale-Conant Corporation, 1995.

Marketing Books

Elkman, Richard. *Building Better Ads*, 5th Edition. BuilderBooks, 1999.

Levinson, Jay Conrad. *Guerrilla Marketing.* Mariner Books, 1998.

Ries, Al and Laura. *22 Immutable Laws of Branding.* HarperCollins, 2002.

Ries, Al, and Jack Trout. *22 Immutable Laws of Marketing.* HarperBusiness, 1994.

Williams, Ray H. *The Wizard of Ads.* Bard Press, 2001.

More Books by Myers Barnes

Available at BuilderBooks.com

From Good to Great in New Home Sales

Myers Barnes

To Myers "From Good to Great" means pushing your beliefs and expanding your way of thinking—to be better and smarter than your competition and to obtain far beyond the results you want. Whether you are at the top of your company or bound and determined to get there, this is the one "cookbook" for success that will earn your seal of approval.

From MBA Publishing, 2002, 182 pp.

Closing Strong:
The Super Sales Handbook

Myers Barnes

A powerful, comprehensive collection of proven strategies—including concise real life situations and actual "dialogue" that you can use to gain an immediate advantage and win more sales.

From MBA Publishing, 1997, 180 pp.

Reach the Top in New Home & Neighborhood Sales

Myers Barnes

Selling onsite in an amenitized community, representing the builder and the developer is unique, rewarding, and profitable . . . if you have a system. Now you can master the strategies used by renowned sales stars with this paint-by-numbers process: custom designed to position home builders, sales professionals and developers with the insight to reach today's purchaser.

From MBA Publishing, 1999, 261 pp.

Index